MW01243440

A Spiritual Interpretation of the Christian Scriptures: the Gospels

As taught by the Unity School of Religious Studies

Rev. James R. D. Yeaw, D.Div., Editor

Unity of Northern Colorado

A Spiritual Interpretation of the Christian Scriptures: the Gospels is a work developed by the Unity School of Religious Studies of the Unity School of Christianity. It has been edited for clarity with notes added pertaining to modern Bible scholarship.

Acknowledgment

This material was prepared for the Correspondence School Department by Herbert J. Hunt, Dean of Bible Studies for the Unity School of Christianity. Dr. Hunt, whose classes in Bible were eagerly attended by ministerial students, teacher-counsellor trainees, and others, brings to his teaching a rich background of experience both in the Unity ministry and at Unity School of Christianity. We are deeply appreciative of the contributions he made to the Unity educational program, and especially we acknowledge the insight and understanding he expressed in these correspondence lessons

First Edition, Second Printing, 2022

Library of Congress Cataloging-in-Publication Data

Yeaw, James, ed.
A Spiritual Interpretation of the Christian Scriptures: the Gospels
 P. cm
Includes index
ISBN-13: 978-1517629038
ISBN-10: 1517629039
Bible
    1. New Testament 2. Metaphysical Bible Interpretation

Contents

Forward – Christian Scriptures – Part I

Purpose

The purpose of this course of lessons is threefold:

(1) to direct us to read and study the books of the Bible, giving us a better understanding of events of the Bible as applied to individual unfoldment;

(2) to furnish historical helps that shed light on the Bible text; and

(3) To provide a key to the spiritual meaning of the Bible as interpreted by Unity.

The course is by no means an exhaustive study of the Christian Scriptures, but it will familiarize us with the outstanding characters and teachings.

This course is in addition to the regular Unity Correspondence School Course and is not required of those training to be licensed Unity teachers. It will, however, be helpful to them and also to those who are now engaged in the Unity ministry.

Required Textbooks

A New Revised Standard Version of the Bible should be acquired. This edition is theologically neutral. It has not been edited and translated with a particular theology in mind. In addition to the Bible with a concordance, a dictionary, and maps are recommended. Bible texts in the lessons are quoted from the NRSV Edition, unless otherwise indicated.

The *Metaphysical Bible Dictionary*, printed by Unity, is an invaluable reference book and should be a part of your working reference library.

Instructions

1. The course consists of twenty-four lessons with ten questions on each lesson. The first five questions of each lesson relate to historical and factual material covered in the Bible. The last five questions refer to metaphysical interpretation.

2. Each lesson gives an assignment from the Bible. Before answering the questions, read and study the designated scriptural passages as given in the assignment for each lesson. This will give you a more comprehensive understanding of the lesson and eliminate the possibility of overlapping subject matter in your answers.

3. Be sure you understand the question. Your answers should be specific and should cover the point thoroughly. No question should be answered by "yes" or "no," or in one sentence. Questions containing several sections should be answered one section at a time, yet totaling one answer. The several sections are given to assist you in adequately covering the question. If a question has an (a) and (b) part, please make a separate paragraph for each part.

4. Please do not include any lengthy quotations, but rather give your own interpretation of the points under consideration. When Bible quotations are used, be sure they are exact. Use quotation marks and give the Bible reference.

5. We recommend that you write out each question as practice in writing the answers in an online test that is electronically scored.

6. Lessons are not required to be completed on any specified schedule. Feel free to take as long as is necessary to study the lesson.

Freewill Offerings

We only charge for the cost of materials and testing. The policy of Unity of Northern Colorado is to place no price on its ministry. In compliance with the ideal and practice of this policy, we offer these lessons on a freewill offering basis.

To you who are seeking knowledge of the Bible and understanding of the meaning it has for you today, these lessons are dedicated. As literature the Bible is among the world's greatest; as a source of spiritual inspiration its message is perpetually contemporary. Our prayer is that your study may take you forward in your search for enlightenment.

Introduction

Before taking up the first lesson in this course, it may be well to remind ourselves of our main purpose. Our purpose is to make a study of the Christian Scriptures[1]— not to study about the Christian Scripture. The difference should be clear. Many books have been written, and many more will be written about the Christian Scriptures; and undoubtedly some of these will prove helpful. But with this multitude of books it is easily possible to gather much information about the Scriptures, and at the same time remain unfamiliar with the contents itself. Therefore in this course, while reference will be made to a number of books, our main emphasis will be upon the contents of the Christian Scriptures.

You will find that as we attain a good grasp of the contents of the Bible, we will be attracted to helpful study books; but until this grasp is attained, the reading of many books may lead to confusion. Hence, the one necessary textbook is a good translation of the Bible. Usually, of course, the Christian Scriptures are bound together with the Hebrew Scriptures, forming the complete Bible. As previously mentioned, Bible texts in the lessons are quoted from the New Revised Standard Version, unless otherwise designated. Various translations are helpful, and may be used for further studies—especially for comparison of certain passages.

---

[1] We use the correct designation here. The Bible is comprised of the Hebrew and Christian Scriptures, a an "old" and a "new" set of writings.

The plan of study for these lessons may be outlined as follows:

After reading through this Introduction, take up the first lesson, together with your Bible, and then:

1. Read carefully the first Bible passage, as given in the first section of the lesson. Do not try at this time to read all the passages given in the lesson—only the passage connected with the first section.

2. When the above reading is completed, read and consider the notes relating to this passage, as given in the lesson. This will help to clear up certain obscure points, and also make the entire passage more understandable.

3. Then read the passage again. This time the reading will prove much more interesting and helpful. Above all, do not hurry in these readings. Better to read a little with understanding, than to read much without attaining such understanding.

4. Following this, read the next passage given in the lesson, and so on; in each case taking the several steps suggested above.

5. After this procedure has been followed, carefully and systematically, to the end of the lesson, you should be in a position to start answering the questions.

However, prior to the suggestions given above, a few words regarding the Bible books to be studied may be in order. In this first part of the Study of the Christian Scriptures we are reading from the Gospels. These cover the life, teachings, and activities of Jesus. The remainder of the Christian Scriptures will be covered in the second part of the course.

The Gospels are four in number, as follows:

Mark
Updated Scholarship

While the gospel is attributed to John Mark, a disciple of Peter, most scholars today give a date of 70-75 CE by an unknown author who is writing to answer questions following the destruction of Jerusalem.[2]

Mark is the shortest and earliest of the Gospels, and was written about 65 CE. Mark (or John Mark, as he is sometimes called) is mentioned in other parts of the Christian Scriptures, and was associated with Barnabas and Paul on their first missionary journey.[3] Later on, Mark attached himself to Peter, as interpreter and secretary.[4] An early writer, about 140 CE, gives the following information regarding the writing of Mark's Gospel:[5]

> *"Mark, having become the interpreter of Peter, wrote down accurately everything that he remembered, without however recording in order what was either said or done by Christ. For neither did he hear the Lord, nor did he follow him, but afterwards, as I said, attended Peter, who adapted his instructions to the needs of his hearers, but had no design of giving a connected account of the*

---

[2] White, J. Benton *From Adam to Armageddon* Wadsworth Publishing, 2005, p. 243
[3] Acts 13:5
[4] See I Peter 5:13
[5] Hastings, James *Dictionary of the Bible*, Baker Books, p. 579

Lord's oracles (or words). So then Mark made no mistake while he thus wrote down some things as he remembered them; for he made it his one care not to omit anything that he heard, nor to set down any false statement therein."

Mark's Gospel is written in a simple, straight-forward manner, and is notable for movement and dramatic effect in its descriptions. The word straight-way, for example, occurs about fifty times. Actually, what we have in this Gospel bears all the marks of an eyewitness account — and this eyewitness seems to have many of those characteristics that we usually associate with Peter.

Matthew
Updated Scholarship

Although some of the content of the Gospel of Matthew is unique to that book, most scholars do not find any evidence that it was compiled by the apostle Matthew and current scholarship dates the book ca 80-90 CE by an unknown author.[6]

Matthew's Gospel has several outstanding features. To begin with, we have here a firsthand account of many of the events recorded—since Matthew, sometimes called Levi, was an actual disciple of Jesus.[7] Then, the style of writing in this Gospel indicates that the writer was a well-educated man, and accustomed to the best forms of public address. There are indications that Matthew wrote down many of the actual sayings of

---

[6] White, J. Benton *From Adam to Armageddon* Wadsworth Publishing, 2005, p. 244
[7] See Matthew 9:9 and Luke 5:27

Jesus—possibly at the time of utterance, or shortly thereafter—and that these "sayings," transcribed onto small slips of parchment or papyrus, circulated freely among the early Christians. However, around 70 CE Matthew, or someone closely associated with him, put these "sayings" into connected form, adding the circumstances surrounding and leading to them, together with other important information, and thus forming our present Gospel according to Matthew.

Matthew's Gospel seems to have been written especially for the Jewish Christians, and therefore it places emphasis upon the messiahship of Jesus. Indeed, the theme of this Gospel might be stated as: "Jesus, the Jewish Messiah." Matthew writes of Jesus as "King of the Jews"; shows that Jesus was connected with the royal line of David; and as a background for the birth of Jesus, he mentions kings, priests, wise men, and other exalted personages. Matthew makes frequent use of Old Testament quotations, and a characteristic phrase, repeated over and over again, is: "That it might be fulfilled."[8]

Luke
Updated Scholarship

Most scholars agree that the author of Luke/Acts was a gentile convert who was a follower of the teachings of Paul. But differences with Paul's letters and the two-source theory (see below) indicate that the books should be dated ca. 90-100/110 CE by an unknown author.[9]

---

[8] Matthew 1:22
[9] White, J. Benton *From Adam to Armageddon* Wadsworth Publishing, 2005, p. 252

Luke was not a disciple of Jesus, but was a convert of the apostle Paul. Thus, the information contained in Luke's Gospel is not of the firsthand type found in Matthew. Luke's information came through the apostle Paul and other early leaders, and through personal research. The "preface" to Luke's Gospel[10] indicates how careful and painstaking Luke was in compiling his Gospel; and it would appear that some part of the material was personally gathered during the two years Luke spent in the vicinity of Jerusalem, while Paul was in prison there.[11] This would be around 57- 59 CE—although the actual Gospel according to Luke was not completed and in circulation until around 70 CE.

Luke, being himself a Gentile, wrote for Gentile Christians, and made his theme: "Jesus, the Savior of Mankind." This universal viewpoint is readily recognized in "sending out the seventy",[12] the parable of the Good Samaritan,[13] and many other passages. Also, when telling of the birth of Jesus, Luke, in contrast with Matthew, uses as a background the humble shepherds and the overcrowded inn, with the birth taking place in the outbuildings of the inn. This does not mean that the stories in Matthew and Luke should be regarded as contradictory. Rather, they are complementary, and together they make one complete picture; for Jesus was both the Messiah of the Jews and also the Savior of mankind. The Gospel of Luke is written in such an interesting and helpful way, and contains so much of what is often termed "the human touch," that it has been designated "the most beautiful book in the world."

---

[10] Luke 1:1-4
[11] See Acts 23-26
[12] Luke 10:1-20
[13] Luke 10:25-37

These three Gospels—Matthew, Mark, and Luke—are sometimes referred to as "the Synoptic Gospels"; we should become familiar with this term. The word synoptic, as used, means "seeing from the same general viewpoint." In other words, the Gospels of Matthew, Mark, and Luke cover similar ground, and have much in common. However, there are also some differences—and it is these similarities and differences that give rise to what is known as "the synoptic problem." This problem may be briefly stated as follows:

1. All three Gospels contain similar material. Indeed, in many instances the same story is told in word-for-word fashion.
2. Practically the whole of Mark's Gospel is reproduced somewhere in Matthew or Luke.
3. However, some material is found in Matthew and Luke which does not appear in Mark.
4. Furthermore, in Matthew and also in Luke there are some stories which are peculiar to these Gospels. Matthew has some material which is found only in Matthew; while Luke also has material which is found only in Luke.

The "problem" is to find an explanation that will satisfactorily cover all the above points; and the suggested solution is briefly as follows:

Mark

3% unique
to Mark

Mark/Matthew		Mark/Luke
94% of Mark	**Matches:**	79% of Mark
55% of Matthew	76% of Mark	42% of Luke
	45% of Matthew	
	23% of Luke	

Matthew

20% unique
to Matthew

Matthew/Luke
70% of Matthew
64% of Luke

Luke

35% unique
to Luke

1. Mark's was the first Gospel to be written (as noted above).
2. At the time when Mark's Gospel was first circulated there were in circulation some strips of parchment, or papyrus, on which appeared some "sayings" of Jesus. These "sayings" were highly prized by the early Christians, who seem to have used them freely at the early church gatherings; and these "sayings" are now technically known under the symbol "Q."
3. Thus, when Matthew and Luke started to write their Gospels, they would have had before them the completed Gospel of Mark, and also some collections of the "sayings of Jesus" ("Q"). The Gospel of Mark and these "sayings" were freely drawn upon by both Matthew and Luke. This would account for points 1, 2, and 3 of the "problem."
4. Both Matthew and Luke also had their own special sources of information—and the material thus at

hand was incorporated by each in his Gospel. This would satisfactorily explain point 4.

Tis brief explanation is given so that you will not be confused by the similarities and differences found in the Synoptic Gospels. Of course, many other theories have been put forward from time to time; but what is given above seems to meet the situation.

John

The Gospel of John stands in a class by itself, and is sometimes referred to as "the Spiritual Gospel." This term should not be regarded as a reflection on the Synoptic Gospels, nor is there any suggestion that they are not of a "spiritual" nature. Rather, the term Spiritual is intended to indicate that there are several marked differences between John's Gospel and the Synoptic Gospels.

John's Gospel was, in all probability, written at Ephesus, sometime between 90 and 120 CE. This makes it of much later date than the Synoptic Gospels. The contents also indicate that John's Gospel was written for what might be termed "advanced students"—that is, those who were already familiar with the Synoptic Gospels.

John's Gospel gives a great deal of what is usually termed "advanced teaching"—such as "the New Birth",[14] "the Bread of Life",[15] "the New Commandment",[16] to mention only a few such teachings. Then, there are the "I AM teachings"—"I am the light of the world",[17] "I am the

---

[14] John 3
[15] John 6
[16] John 15
[17] John 8:12

resurrection, and the life",[18] and many similar passages. These "I AM teachings" do not appear in the Synoptic Gospels.

John's Gospel does not contain parables, such as are found in the Synoptic Gospels. However, it will be noticed that the writer of John's Gospel frequently uses miracles to illustrate certain important teachings, instead of parables. Thus, we have the teaching, "I am the Light of the world"—and following is the account of healing the man born blind.[19] Then there is the teaching, "I am the bread of life"—closely followed by the miracle of feeding the five thousand;[20] and there are several other instances of this sort. However, all this will be fully explained in a later lesson.

The Synoptic Gospels record the Sermon on the Mount, in various forms—and this apparently covers teaching given during the earlier part of Jesus' ministry. In contrast with this, John's Gospel gives us the "Upper Room discourses"[21] — and these were given at the close of Jesus' ministry.

Thus, John's Gospel gives us not only the "facts" of Jesus' ministry, but also the interpretation of many of his teachings and activities. Indeed, the writer of this Gospel sums up the entire record of the life and teachings of Jesus Christ in a clear statement of purpose: [22]

----

[18] John 11:25
[19] John 8-9
[20] John 6
[21] John 14-17
[22] John 20:31

These are written, that ye may believe that Jesus is the Christ, the Son of God; and that believing ye may have life in his name.

We are now ready to take up the first regular lesson.

Chapter 1 - The Birth of Jesus, the Christ

Questions

Historical Questions:

1. When and where was Jesus born? Who was the Jewish king at this time? Which synoptic Gospels record this important event? Give chapter and verse references.

2. Briefly explain how John's Gospel deals with the birth of Jesus. (John 1:1-14)

3. What was Herod's attitude following the visit of the Wise Men? What action did Herod take when the wise men failed to return to him?

4. Where did Jesus live before beginning his public ministry? Give a reference to substantiate your answer.

5. In your own words, briefly tell of Jesus' visit to Jerusalem, when he was about twelve years of age. (Luke 2:40-52)

Metaphysical Questions:

1. What does the name "Jesus" mean? (Matt. 1:21) Explain briefly what this means to us.

2. Who were the Wise Men? (Matt. 2:1-12) What do they represent in our experience?

3. What does Herod represent in consciousness? Explain briefly how this operates in our life and affairs.

4. What does Mary the mother of Jesus symbolize? How does this affect us today?

5. Briefly explain why the teaching of the Virgin Birth is important to us. How is this teaching connected with Matt. 5:8?

Lesson Text

Reading: Matthew 2:1-23.

The second chapter of Matthew's Gospel opens with these words: "Now when Jesus was born in Bethlehem of Judea[23] ..." This statement immediately directs our thought to a very important event in history, Vis: the coming of Jesus. In this first lesson, therefore, we shall deal not only with this event, but also with a number of important considerations arising therefrom. The date usually given for the birth of Jesus is 4 BCE.

The following notes should help toward a better understanding of the first Scripture reading given above:

The Wise Men

While it is customary to refer to "the Three Wise Men," we should note that Scripture does not indicate any number, but simply states that "Wise men from the east came to Jerusalem".[24] The idea that there were three wise men seems to have arisen sometime during the fifth century — probably from the fact that there were three

---

[23] Early Christian traditions describe Jesus as being born in Bethlehem: in one, a verse in the Book of Micah is interpreted as a prophecy that the Messiah would be born there. The Christian Scriptures have two different accounts of the birth. In the Gospel of Luke, Jesus' parents live in Nazareth and travel for the Census of Quirinius to Bethlehem, where Jesus is born, after which they return home. In the Gospel of Matthew version, which takes place at least a decade earlier during the reign of Herod the Great, there is no mention of the census and the family are living in Bethlehem. Told that a 'King of the Jews' has been born in the town, Herod orders the killing of all the boys aged two and under in the town and surrounding area. Joseph, warned of this in a dream, flees to Egypt with his family and later settle in Nazareth. Most modern biographers of Herod doubt the massacre was a real event.
[24] Matthew 2:1

gifts. However, it must be recognized that this is not an entirely satisfactory method of reasoning! An early writer suggests that these wise men were really kings, coming to pay homage to the King of Kings. The story was further embellished in the eighth century, when names were given to these wise men: Kaspar, Belshazzar, and Melchior. But it should be noted that nothing of this sort has place in the actual Scripture story.

Perhaps the important teaching in this passage may be summed up in the sentence, "Wise men ever seek the Christ." Applied to ourselves this means that when our God-given wisdom is spiritually illumined, we seek the Christ—not in some far-off place, but at the center of our being. The star, or spiritual illumination, leads us to the realization of "Christ in you, the hope of glory".[25]

Herod and the Star

Many attempts have been made to identify the star mentioned in this story. The most popular explanation associates the star with a periodic appearance of "Halley's Comet"; and calculations have been made which would indicate that this comet may have appeared about the time of Jesus' birth. However, we should not overlook one very important feature in the story: while the star was clearly visible to the wise men, neither Herod nor his followers could see it. Had the star been visible to Herod, he would not have been forced to depend upon the Wise Men for information regarding the whereabouts of the newborn King. Why was this star visible to the Wise Men, and not to Herod? Probably the best answer is to be found

---

[25] Colossians 1:27

in the oft-quoted phrase, "Spiritual things must be spiritually discerned." In other words, the spiritually illumined Wise Men were able to discern the guiding light, while Herod, the un-illumined, could see nothing out of the ordinary in the skies.

Metaphysically, Herod represents "the ruling will of the physical ego in sense consciousness".[26] We sometimes speak of this in terms of personal will; and when personal will takes command, we are usually led into ways of fear, jealousy, cruelty, and destruction. Note Herod's attitude and actions following the visit of the Wise Men.[27] Personal will, in like manner, fears the possibility of displacement, and seeks to "kill out" every good thought and purpose arising within our consciousness. Fortunately, there is a Power which directs us to take our thoughts and purposes "into Egypt," beyond the destructive intentions of Herod.

Read the passage: Luke 2:1-39.

Shepherds, Angels

Luke's account of the birth of Jesus stands in contrast to that given by Matthew. In place of the high and important personages, we have just a few humble shepherds, feeding their flocks. Luke writes: "And there were shepherds ... abiding in the field, and keeping watch by night over their flock".[28] Perhaps it is worthy of note that in this instance we do not find ourselves wondering whether there were three, or thirty shepherds as we did

---

[26] *Metaphysical Bible Dictionary*, p. 274
[27] Matthew 2:16-18
[28] Luke 2:8

with the Wise Men; nor are we concerned about enrolling the names of these shepherds in a spiritual "Who's Who"! Nevertheless, these humble shepherds sought and found the Christ, even as did the wise men.

It should be further noted that these shepherds had their moments of illumination, even as did the Wise Men; for not only did the "glory of the Lord" shine around them, but they also heard the angelic chorus: *"Glory to God in the highest, and on earth peace, good will toward men"*[29] [30]

Personal Application

While we may learn much from the action of the Wise Men,[31] there is also a helpful lesson in the story of the shepherds, and this may be stated briefly as follows:

As we carefully "shepherd" our thoughts, there may come to us moments of spiritual illumination, and we may be directed to the Christ Child. However, note how the shepherds in the story did not stop with illumination; they said, "Let us go now even unto Bethlehem, and see this thing that is come to pass".[32] In other words, their "hearing" and "seeing" were followed by "doing"—and it was because of this that they made actual contact with the Christ Child. Surely this means something to us!

---

[29] Luke 2:14

[30] This quotation is from the King James, or Authorized, Version. This passage is somewhat difficult to translate, hence the many variations. However, the Authorized Version seems to have caught the poetic beauty of this passage, and this more than atones for any inaccuracy of translation.

[31] Matthew 2

[32] Luke 2:15

Simeon and Anna

Be sure to read this section carefully, and especially note the beautiful little poem, as given by Simeon.[33]

Read the passages: Matthew 1:1-25; Luke 3:23-38; Luke 1:26-56

The Genealogies

Many readers of the Christian Scriptures are puzzled by the inclusion of these "family trees" in the story of the birth of Jesus. We usually think of Jesus as being "born of the Virgin Mary"—and the Gospel writers place considerable emphasis on this point; but these lists deal, not with Mary, but with the family of Joseph. Why should this be?

The explanation is found in the fact that Mary, at the time of the birth of Jesus, was betrothed to Joseph;[34] because of this, Mary was then legally a member of the house of Joseph. Thus, while Jesus was actually born "of" Mary, yet at the same time he was born "into" the house of Joseph. It was because of this that Jesus was recognized as being "of the line of David."

An important difference should be noted between these two genealogies: Matthew traces the line back to Abraham, through David. This gives emphasis to Matthew's theme of Jesus as the Jewish Messiah, since there was general agreement that the Messiah should come through the line of David. Luke, however, traces the line beyond Abraham, and takes it back to Adam. This is

---

[33] Luke 2:28-32
[34] Matthew 1:18

done because the theme of Luke's Gospel is "Jesus, the Savior of Mankind"; and by tracing the line back to Adam, the writer established the connection between Jesus and the entire human race; for Luke regards Jesus not only as the Messiah of the Jewish people, but also as the Savior of the whole world.

The Virgin Birth

When considering the subject of the Virgin Birth of Jesus, two important points should be kept well in mind.

First; the story of the Virgin Birth is clearly presented in two of the Synoptic Gospels.[35] Mark does not record the birth of Jesus, but starts his story with the beginning of Jesus' ministry. Both Matthew and Luke set forth the facts in clear, unmistakable terms. Hence, the story of the Virgin Birth must have been current among, and accepted by, the early Christians—since both these Gospels were in circulation around A.D. 70.

However, the second point seems somewhat paradoxical: it would appear that the Virgin Birth was not openly discussed during the active ministry of Jesus. If there had been any discussion of this sort, surely there would be some indication in the Gospel records. But Jesus was known as "the Carpenter," or "the Teacher"—not as "the One miraculously born." Indeed, the people of Nazareth, the hometown of Jesus, are reported as saying, "Is not this Joseph's son?"[36] We may ask, then: Why is the Virgin Birth not mentioned in the stories of Jesus' ministry as given in the gospels? The explanation might easily be

---

[35] Matthew 1:1-25 and Luke 1:26-56
[36] Luke 4:22

that Jesus desired that his teaching should stand on its own merits, rather than as coming from someone "miraculously born." Jesus' emphasis was upon Truth, and not upon any claim of miraculous birth. Thus, Luke informs us that Mary "kept all these sayings in her heart"[37] — apparently withholding all this type of information until the time was right.

The question may now arise as to why the story of the Virgin Birth is given in the opening sections of the Gospels. Was it an effort on the part of the Gospel writers to prove the divinity of Jesus? Or was it evidence put forward to show that Jesus was "different"? Scarcely! In point of fact, the Gospels contain many passages which lay stress upon Jesus' similarity to us, rather than upon being "different." Jesus was tempted, hungry, thirsty, and shared all our human experiences. Jesus also gave instructions that we are to follow him. But how could we follow if he were "different"? We would be hopelessly handicapped right at the very start!

It would seem, therefore, that the story of the Virgin Birth is given in the Gospels to bring before us a very important lesson. Again and again, especially at Christmastime, we hear the lines quoted:

Though Christ a thousand times in Bethlehem be born, if he's not born in thee, thy soul is all forlorn.

But the Christ can be born in us only as we develop the virgin state of mind—the one-pointed consciousness wherein we recognize "God only," and are ready to say,

---

[37] Luke 2:51

with Mary, "Behold, the handmaid of the Lord; be it unto me according to thy word".[38] Jesus himself emphasized this when he said to Nicodemus, "Ye must be born anew".[39] Paradoxical as it may appear, we ourselves must be "born anew" before the Christ can be born in us. This is the virgin state of mind. A somewhat similar teaching is found in the Sermon on the Mount, where Jesus said, "Blessed are the pure in heart: for they shall see God".[40]

When studying the teaching of the Virgin Birth, it is well to keep in mind the metaphysical meaning of the name "Mary." In the Christian Scriptures several women by this name are mentioned; and in practically all instances these may be interpreted as having bearing upon the emotional, or loving side of our nature. Thus, we should recognize love as an important factor in the new birth. Regarding Mary, the mother of Jesus, the Metaphysical Dictionary states:

> "Mary, the mother of Jesus, represents the soul that magnifies the Lord 'daily in the temple' and through its devotions prepares itself for the higher life. She signifies the divine motherhood of love. ... The coming of the Christ body into activity is the result of an exalted idea sown in the mind and matured by the soul (Mary). The soul is devout and expectant. It believes in the so-called miraculous as a possibility. Mary expected the birth of the Messiah, according to the promise of the Holy Spirit. She was

---

[38] Luke 1:38
[39] John 3:7
[40] Matthew 5:8

overshadowed by that high idea ... and what is called the birth of Christ took place".[41]

Read the passage: Luke 2:40-52

The "Silent Years"

Many find themselves wondering about the activities of Jesus prior to the time when he entered upon his public ministry. Matthew tells us how Joseph took Mary and the child Jesus into Galilee, "and dwelt in a city called Nazareth".[42] Luke also records how, some twelve years later, Joseph and Mary made a brief visit to Jerusalem, taking Jesus with them.[43] Apart from these two references, there is no direct mention of further activities. The Christian Scriptures indicate that when Jesus entered upon his public ministry he was about thirty years of age.[44] What, then, was he doing during those intervening years?

Some writers have suggested that sometime during those "silent years" Jesus visited other lands, and conversed with religious leaders of that time, thereby gaining valuable information which he later incorporated into his teaching. Such suggestions are interesting; and therefore it may be well to look into the situation, and carefully weigh the evidence.

First of all, it is quite clear that the Gospel writers make no mention of any such journeys. Luke, who tells us that he made careful inquiries concerning all the activities

---

[41] Metaphysical Bible Dictionary, pp. 427-28
[42] Matthew 2:22-23
[43] Luke 2:40-52
[44] Luke 3:23

of Jesus, certainly would have mentioned these journeys to other lands, if he had known anything of them. Any indication of Jesus' visiting other lands and conversing with Gentile teachers would have given additional emphasis to Luke's theme: "Jesus, Savior of Mankind." But apparently Luke knew nothing of such journeys.

It must also be recognized that the Jewish people of that time did not look favorably upon teachers connected with other religions. The Jews believed that they alone had the supreme revelation in their sacred books, and therefore it would have been unthinkable to look to foreigners for further light and guidance. Moreover, Jesus himself rejected all suggestions regarding outside influence upon his teaching. He claimed that his knowledge and teaching came direct from "the Father."

The Gospels contain no indications of extensive journeys to the outside world by Jesus. But the Gospels do contain many indications that those "silent years" were spent within the bounds of the Holy Land. For example, it is recorded that people spoke of Jesus, not as "the great traveler," but as "the Man from Nazareth." Luke 4:16 reads: "And he came to Nazareth, where he had been brought up." John 1:46 records that Nathaniel, speaking of Jesus, said, "Can any good thing come out of Nazareth?" There are several other passages in the Gospels which closely identify Jesus with early activities in Nazareth. Furthermore, the illustrations Jesus used in his talks were all drawn from the life and activities of people in the Holy Land. And Jesus himself once summed up the entire situation by saying: "I was not sent but unto the lost sheep of the house of Israel".[45]

The question may then be asked: What was Jesus actually doing in Nazareth during those "silent years"? The answer is not hard to find. It would appear that Joseph died while Jesus was yet in his teens, and Jesus thereupon became responsible for the support of Mary and the entire family (there being by this time several other children to be cared for. Jesus, during this period, continued to work as a carpenter; and the recognition of his craftsmanship continued even into his public ministry. Then, in addition to these family responsibilities, Jesus must have spent considerable time and effort in preparing himself for his ministry. While there is no record of Jesus' actually entering upon any course of formal theological education, it must be recognized that his mastery of the Hebrew Scriptures was outstanding. Again and again in his later ministry Jesus used Scripture in a way that clearly indicated much careful, painstaking study and research; and all this would have been accompanied by long periods of meditation and prayer. It will prove very helpful if you look out for some of these important "quotes" in subsequent lessons. Certainly, those "silent years" must have been very busy years.

Read the passage: John 1:1-18

Opening the Bible at the first chapter of John, we immediately recognize that we are in an entirely different world as compared with that of the Synoptic Gospels. John

---

[45] Matthew 15:24

does not give details regarding the birth of Jesus, as do Matthew and Luke, but presents his story in metaphysical language. The synoptists tell us that Jesus was born in a certain place, and at a certain time. John, however, goes beyond these "facts" and states:

> In the beginning was the Word ... and the Word was God ... and the Word became flesh, and dwelt among us (and we beheld his glory, glory as of the only begotten from the Father), full of grace and truth.[46]

Thus, we quickly discover why this Gospel is termed "the Spiritual Gospel."

The following notes will prove helpful when reading the complete passage, as mentioned above. However, at this time it will be well to concentrate upon the sections referring to the coming of Jesus.

"In the beginning was the Word [Logos]".[47]

"Logos is the Christ, the Son, the divine Light, the living Word, or Word of the Supreme, and it contains all potentiality; all things were made by it (him). We can appropriate all, or a part, as we choose. Jesus expressed it in all its fullness, and he became the Logos, or Word, made flesh. In other words, Jesus so unified himself in thought, word, and deed with this inner Christ, Logos, Word, creative principle of God, in which are all the ideas in Divine Mind—life, substance, intelligence, wisdom, love, strength, power, that even his seemingly mortal or flesh

---

[46] John 1:1, 14
[47] John 1:1

body took on the divine nature and became immortal, was wholly transformed into God-likeness, spirituality; thus throughout his entire being Jesus showed forth the glory and perfection of God. Those who follow him can make this full attainment that he made, if they accept, as he did, the all-possibility of the Principle".[48]

Make a careful comparison between John 1:1-18 and Genesis 1; 2:1-4. Genesis gives the account of the first creation, while John 1:1-18 leads us into an understanding of the new creation.

"And the Word became Flesh"[49]

> *Jesus recognized this truth that the Christ, the divine-idea man or Word of God, was his true self and that he was consequently the Son of God. Because Jesus held to this perfect image of the divine man, the Christ or Word entered consciously into every atom of his being, even to the very cells of his outer organism, and transformed all his body into pure, immortal, spiritual substance and life. Thus, 'the Word became flesh' "[50]*

After carefully considering all the above sections, following the plan of study suggested in the Introduction, you should now be ready to answer the questions for this lesson.

---

[48] *Metaphysical Bible Dictionary*, pp. 404-05
[49] John 1:14
[50] Fillmore, Charles *Mysteries of John*, p. 15

Chapter 2 - John the Baptizer

Historical Questions:

1. Using your own words, tell briefly the story of John the Baptizer's birth. Bring out some of the outstanding features, just as though you were writing a newspaper report of this important happening.

2. "What was the great message of John the Baptizer? Mention some of the methods he adopted to give special emphasis to this message.

3. What did John the Baptizer say about Jesus? Quote some actual statements, with Scripture references, and a brief explanation of each.

4. How would you explain John the Baptizer as a fulfillment of the popular expectation regarding the reappearance of Elijah?

5. Why was John the Baptizer put in prison? Briefly explain the circumstances, and state what finally happened to him. Did John's tragic death mark the end of the Baptizer movement?

Metaphysical Questions:

1. What does John the Baptizer represent in our consciousness? Explain fully.

2. How is intellectual consciousness related to spiritual consciousness? Explain briefly how a study of John the Baptizer helps us to understand this relationship.

3. What is meant by the statement: "he must increase, but I must decrease" (John 3:30)? How does this apply in our experience?

4. Explain briefly the connection between water baptism and denial.

5. What is meant by the term forerunner as applied to John the Baptizer? How is this related to our own spiritual development?

Lesson Text

In the opening sections of all four Gospels, reference is made to the activities of John the Baptizer. These activities are recorded as a sort of preface, or introduction, to the work of Jesus. Indeed, John the Baptizer is presented in the Gospels as "a man sent from God" to be the forerunner of Jesus. The early part of the Christian Scriptures show how John's preaching and his baptizing "in water" did much to prepare the way for the One who was to baptize "in the Holy Spirit."

You should therefore seek to become well acquainted with the story of John the Baptizer—not only because of John's important place in history, but also for what he represents in our own spiritual development.

One of the best ways of studying the life and activities of John the Baptizer is to arrange the story in acrostic form—using each separate letter of the word Baptizer as a heading for one of the sections to be studied. In this way, each letter of the word will represent an important phase of the life story of John the Baptizer. You will find that this method will not only prove most interesting, but it will also help him to keep all the important factors well in mind.

The acrostic for John the Baptizer will therefore read as follows:

B—Birth of John the Baptizer

Read the passages: Luke 1:5-24; 57-80

In ancient times there was a familiar saying to the effect that an extraordinary man must be born in an extraordinary way. The early Christians—first readers of the Gospels—would have known of this saying and would therefore have delighted in the story of the birth of John the Baptizer; for he was indeed born in an extraordinary way. Note some of the extraordinary circumstances and happenings connected with his birth:

1. John the Baptizer was born of aged parents. The gospel record indicates that Zacharias and Elizabeth had long ago given up any idea of having a son. Actually, the situation is somewhat similar to that of Abraham and Sarah and the birth of their son Isaac.[51]

2. Then there was the visit of the angel Gabriel to Zacharias, just as the aged priest was about to offer incense at the Temple altar. At that time Zacharias was stricken dumb because of his inability to accept this promise of a son.

3. The forthcoming son was to have a special name—John—even though the regular family names were altogether different.

4. Some extraordinary predictions were made concerning this coming son. The angel said: "he

---

[51] Genesis 18-21

shall be great in the sight of the Lord, and ... be filled with the Holy Spirit".[52]

5. When the son was born, and named, Zacharias bad his speech restored. With his newly-freed tongue, Zacharias uttered some prophetic words:[53]

Yea and thou, child, shall be called the prophet of the Most High: for thou shalt go before the face of the Lord to make ready his ways; to give knowledge of salvation unto his people in the remission of their sins, because of the tender mercy of our God, whereby the dayspring from on high shall visit us, to shine upon them that sit in darkness and the shadow of death; to guide our feet into the way of peace.

We are told further:[54]

And the child grew, and waxed strong in spirit, and was in the deserts till the day of his showing unto Israel.

A—Activities of John the Baptizer

Read the passages: Matthew 3:1-12; Mark 1:1-8; Luke 3:1-20; John 1:6-7; 19-28

---

[52] Luke 1:15
[53] Luke 1:76-79
[54] Luke 1:80

After reading the above passages, give careful consideration to the following important points:

1. John the Baptizer's appearance. His dress was distinctive, and dated back to much earlier times. This would tend to remind the people of the tradition regarding the return of Elijah.

2. John the Baptizer's message. John proclaimed, "Repent ye; for the kingdom of heaven is at hand".[55] It is important to recognize what was intended by this announcement. Undoubtedly this had reference to the coming of the Messiah; but this "day of the Lord" would be a time of terror, rather than of rejoicing. Wrongdoers would be severely punished, and only those who were truly righteous would escape. Hence, John's message would be understood to mean, "Repent—or else!" According to John's teaching, repentance and a radical change in all life's activities (particularly when those activities were not in accord with the scriptural law) would be the only way to escape this retribution from "on high."

3. John the Baptizer and Elijah. Some find themselves somewhat puzzled because of the seeming contradiction between John 1:20 and Matthew 11:14.

4. As mentioned above, the Jewish people at that time believed that the coming of the long-expected Messiah would be preceded by the re-appearance of Elijah. Jesus referred to and explained this popular expectation, as recorded in Matthew

---

[55] Matthew 3:2

11:11-15. This indicates that Jesus saw in John the Baptizer those Elijah-like qualities which met current expectations, even though the Jewish leaders could not see them. By way of illustration, we may see something similar in our own experience. Perhaps at a time of political crisis somebody may say, "What we need now is another Washington, or another Lincoln!" And we understand such a statement to mean that we are looking for, and hoping for the appearance of some person having those helpful qualities that we associate with Washington or Lincoln. In a somewhat similar way, Jesus saw in John the Baptizer a coming forth of the forceful speech and positive actions of Elijah.

5. However, looking at the words of John the Baptizer, as recorded in John 1:19-21, we must recognize that here is a statement of literal fact. John the Baptizer was not Elijah; neither was Elijah John the Baptizer. Moreover, John the Baptizer would not publicly claim that he possessed the power and other qualities of Elijah. Such a claim would hinder rather than help his work. We should also recognize that John the Baptizer, despite his austere manner, was at heart a very humble man. This is made clear in his attitude toward Jesus, especially at the baptism. Nevertheless, others recognized in John the Baptizer what he would not claim for himself. Jesus was among those who recognized John the Baptizer as a truly great man, for Jesus said, "Among them that are born of

women there hath not arisen a greater than John the Baptizer".[56]

6. John the Baptizer's acknowledgment of Jesus as the Messiah. Not only did John proclaim: "he that cometh after me is mightier than I ... he shall baptize you in the Holy Spirit and in fire",[57] but he also pointed to Jesus as the fulfillment of this prediction.[58]

7. John the Baptizer's connection with the Essenes. It is quite possible that John the Baptizer, prior to his public ministry, was influenced in some degree by the Essenes. His austere teaching, and his emphasis upon the coming "day of the Lord," closely follow the Essene teaching. However, it would also seem that John the Baptizer disagreed with the Essenes on at least one important point. The Essenes taught and practiced exclusiveness and withdrawal from the ordinary activities of life. But John, instead of withdrawing, went direct to the people and taught them to apply the teaching in all matters of everyday life. John the Baptizer preached reform, rather than apartness.

P—Prisoner (John the Baptizer in prison)

Read the passage: Mark 6:17-29

---

[56] Matthew 11:11
[57] Matthew 3:11
[58] See John 1:29-36

Mark's account makes interesting reading, and indicates the personal factor behind the arrest and execution of John the Baptizer. However, Josephus, the Jewish historian, suggests that John was arrested for political reasons. According to Josephus, Herod feared that John's preaching concerning the "coming One" would lead to insurrection. This, in turn, might lead to the dethronement of Herod himself and the destruction of his kingdom.

T—Troubled and Tempted (John the Baptizer in difficulty)

Read the passage: Matthew 11:2-15

Reading between the lines in this passage, we can sense that when John the Baptizer was thrust into prison, he expected that Jesus would exercise his power and bring about a miraculous release. But this hoped-for release did not materialize; and therefore John began to have doubts. Could he have been mistaken in Jesus? Was Jesus really the Messiah, or must there be a further period of waiting? Actually, at this time John seems to have been tempted to the point of abandoning his recognition of Jesus as Messiah.

We should carefully note Jesus' reply to John's question. Jesus did not give the messengers a plain yes or no. Instead, he suggested that they look around and observe the type of work he was doing, and then draw their own conclusions. Actually, Jesus was here quoting indirectly from Isaiah 35:5-6 and 61:1. Since these Scripture passages were then regarded as referring to the type of work the Messiah would do upon his arrival, and since Jesus himself was accomplishing all that was indicated in these passages, it must follow that Jesus was definitely the Messiah.

It should be further noted that, notwithstanding this wavering on the part of John the Baptizer, Jesus still held him in highest esteem. Matt. 11:7-11 reports Jesus as saying, in effect, that while Jewish history contained the names of many outstanding men, none of these was greater than John the Baptizer. Truly, an outstanding testimony!

I—Interpretation (John the Baptizer and his baptism)

John the Baptizer signifies a high intellectual perception of Truth, but one not yet quickened of Spirit. John represents that attitude of mind in which we are zealous for the rule of Spirit. This attitude is not spiritual, but a perception of spiritual possibilities and an activity in making conditions in which Spirit may rule. This John-the-Baptizer perception of Truth leads us to strive with evil as a reality, not having discerned the truth about its transitory character.[59]

John the Baptizer may also be said to be that innate principle in us all who ever seeks to do right. Its origin cannot be located—it comes out of the wilderness. It is crude—it is like a voice in the wilderness crying for the right way. The whole human family is naturally true and

---

[59] *Metaphysical Bible Dictionary* Entry: John

honest, and this rugged reformer is a child of nature. Culture does not make people honest nor bring out their natural virtues. The inner soul consciousness that draws its nourishment from nature's storehouse opens the way for the advent of Spirit."[60]

> "Intellectual understanding comes first in the soul's development, then a deeper understanding of principle follows, until the whole man ripens into wisdom."[61]

> "In the regeneration two states of mind are constantly at work. First comes the cleansing or denial state, in which all the error thoughts are eliminated. This includes forgiveness for sins committed and a general clearing up of the whole consciousness. The idea is to get back into the pure, natural consciousness of Spirit. This state of mind is typified by John the Baptizer, who came out of the wilderness a child of nature whose mission it was to make straight the way for the one who was to follow.

> "This putting away of sin from the consciousness (baptism through denial, plus forgiveness) is very closely allied to the deeper work that is to follow; so much so that to the observer it seems the same. Hence the followers of John, when they saw the works he did, asked if he was the Messiah. His

---

[60] *Metaphysical Bible Dictionary*, p. 357
[61] Fillmore, Charles *Keep a True Lent*, p. 155

answer was that the One who followed him was to baptize with Holy Spirit'.[62]

S—Spread of the work.

Read the passages: John 3:22-24 and 4:1; Acts 18:24-26 and 19:1-6

From a casual reading of the opening chapters in the Christian Scriptures, we may get the impression that the work of John the Baptizer covered only two or three years, and was limited to the area immediately adjoining Jerusalem. Actually, however, the John-the-Baptizer movement spread to many parts of the then-known world, and continued for many years after John's death. Indeed, the leaders in the early Christian church often encountered men and women who had expectations of a coming Messiah, but who thus far knew "only the baptism of John."

In the Christian Scripture passages given above, we have:

1. An indication of the continuing activity of John the Baptizer, after the ministry of Jesus had begun. Indeed, the two ministries appear here as competitive activities.[63]
2. Acts 18:24-26 deals with something taking place about twenty-five years after the activities mentioned above—and this indicates how the

---

[62] Fillmore, Charles *Mysteries of John*, p. 16-17
[63] John 3:22-24 and 4:1

John-the-Baptizer movement had spread during those intervening years. The Apollos here mentioned came from Alexandria, in Egypt—a city famous for its ancient university; and since Apollos is described as being "an eloquent man … mighty in the scriptures," we may assume that he was a well-educated man. However, the interesting feature is that he is also described as "knowing only the baptism of John." This may indicate that the teaching of John the Baptizer had penetrated into the University of Alexandria; at least, the teaching must have gone far beyond the environs of Jerusalem.

3. Acts 19:1-6 definitely states that the John-the-Baptizer movement had reached as far as Ephesus, in Asia Minor; for in this passage we read of a "study group" which had been organized in that city. Whether this was the result of the labors of Apollos, or whether other teachers had been active, is not quite clear; this is, at least, another indication of the far-reaching effects of the John-the-Baptizer teaching. The members of this "study group" were re-baptized by the Apostle Paul, and they later became part of the Christian group in Ephesus.

T—Tragedy or Triumph?

In closing this study of the life and activities of John the Baptizer, it may be well to attempt some sort of evaluation of the work accomplished.

At first glance, the story of John the Baptizer's life may seem to resolve itself into something of a tragedy. To start so well ... to undertake such an important, God-given work ... to be the forerunner of Jesus Christ—but then to end it all in such an inglorious way! Mark 6:27-29 tells of John's execution: "And when his disciples heard thereof, they came and took up his corpse, and laid it in a tomb." Certainly, all this seems like a tragedy.

But if we take a few moments to list some of the actual accomplishments of John the Baptizer, what at first seems like a tragedy may turn out to be a real triumph. Note the following:

1. John the Baptizer completed his mission as the forerunner of Jesus Christ. In this he stirred up religious interest, which had become dormant. He revived the messianic expectancy among the people, by proclaiming: "Repent; for the kingdom of heaven is at hand".[64] He publicly pointed to Jesus as the "coming One."[65]
2. John the Baptizer fulfilled two very important popular expectations:
    - "Behold, I send my messenger, and he shall prepare the way before me".[66]
    - The reappearance of Elijah.[67]
3. John the Baptizer started what may be termed a "chain reaction," which provided (either directly

---

[64] Matthew 3:2
[65] See John 1:29-34
[66] Matthew 3:1
[67] See Matthew 11:14

or indirectly) six important disciples for Jesus Christ: Andrew and John; Peter and James; Philip and Nathanael.[68]

4. John the Baptizer brought to a close the old order, and opened the way for the new order. The old way of "Moses and the law" gave place to the new way of "grace and truth" through Jesus Christ.[69]

---

[68] See John 1:35-51
[69] See John 1:17

Chapter 3 - Jesus Prepares for His ministry

Historical Questions

1. Why was Jesus baptized? Mention several important reasons for this ceremony.

2. In what way, or ways, did the baptism of Jesus differ from other baptisms performed by John the Baptizer at that time? Were there also some similarities?

3. Explain briefly why Jesus' baptism was immediately followed by a period of temptation.

4. Can you trace a connection between the first temptation, and a question which would arise at the start of Jesus' active ministry? What was the quotation from Deuteronomy which Jesus used at that time?

5. Explain briefly how the second and third temptations were related to the messianic expectations at the time of Jesus. How did Jesus deal with these temptations? Quote some actual statements made by Jesus at this time.

Metaphysical Questions

1. What does baptism represent in our experience?

2. Is an outer ceremony sufficient in itself, or must something else be added? Illustrate your answer from the story of Jesus' baptism.

3. Explain briefly the connection between baptism and the work of denials and affirmations.

4. Can you suggest any reason, or reasons, why a high spiritual experience (such as that which occurred at the baptism of Jesus) should be followed by a period of "temptation"?

5. Explain briefly the step-by-step method of overcoming temptation, as used by Jesus. Can we follow this method today? What good may we gain during these testing periods?

Lesson Text
Read the passages: Matt. 3:13-17; Mark 1:9-11; Luke 3:21-23; John 1:26-34

The Baptism
These passages of Scripture, while differing in some details, bring out the main features in the baptism of Jesus. Check the following:

1. Jesus was baptized by John the Baptizer;
2. John was apparently reluctant to perform this ceremony—which reluctance was overcome by the reassuring words of Jesus;
3. the baptism apparently followed the same form of immersion used for other candidates for baptism;
4. however, following the baptism of Jesus there was the manifestation of the Holy Spirit (which did not appear to others) "descending as a dove ... upon him";[70]
5. There was also the divine message, "This is my beloved Son, in whom I am well pleased".[71]

---

[70] Matthew 3:16
[71] Matthew 3:17

After giving careful consideration to the above, the questions may arise: Why was Jesus baptized? What was Jesus' purpose in going through this ceremony?

Of course, we cannot regard Jesus' baptism as a sign of repentance, symbolizing the washing away of sin. Matthew's account tells how other people came to John "confessing their sins",[72] but we always think of Jesus as "the sinless One." Indeed, later in his ministry Jesus himself laid emphasis upon this very point, when he said, "Which of you convicts me of sin?"[73] Neither should we see in the baptism an indication that Jesus was thereby joining the John-the-Baptizer movement. The Gospels make clear that at quite an early period Jesus completely disassociated himself from the John-the-Baptizer movement.[74] This will be further discussed in a later lesson.

Seeking to understand the meaning of Jesus' baptism, we find several things standing out clearly:

1. The baptism may be regarded as a public declaration by Jesus of his intention to enter upon his active ministry. The gospel writers make a special point of associating the baptism with the opening of Jesus' ministry.[75] Nowadays, the start of a minister's active work is usually marked by some form of ordination ceremony. The baptism of Jesus may therefore be regarded as fulfilling a somewhat similar function. Indeed, in all probability Jesus was

---

[72] Matthew 3:6
[73] John 8:46
[74] John 4:1-2
[75] Mark 1:1 and Luke 3:23

referring to this when he said, "It becomes us to fulfil all righteousness".[76]

2. The baptism may also be regarded as a symbol of something Jesus was actually doing at that time. While there was no thought of "washing away sin"—as already indicated—yet Jesus was actually letting go of one form of activity and entering upon an entirely different form of life. Thus far Jesus had been a carpenter, a shaper of wood; now he was to become a shaper of men. He was also letting go of the sheltered family life and launching out into the world, with "not where to lay his head".[77] He was letting go of family responsibilities, but taking upon himself worldwide responsibilities. Perhaps, also, Jesus saw in this baptism a foreshadowing of that baptism which he was to experience later, as mentioned to his disciples: "Are ye able ... to be baptized with the baptism that I am baptized with?"[78]

3. But may it not be that Jesus, through his baptism, was also seeking to present to us some very important lessons? Note how the emphasis in the baptism story is placed not upon the outer ceremony, but upon the descending of the Holy Spirit. This means that while outer forms and ceremonies may have their place, they are not really complete in themselves. The "outward and visible sign" must be followed by a receiving of the

---

[76] Matthew 3:15
[77] Matthew 8:20
[78] Mark 10:38

"inward spiritual grace." Baptism may be regarded as a symbol of cleansing, or letting go; but this is only preparatory to receiving or taking hold of the desired good. John baptized with water; following the example of Jesus, we should seek to be baptized in the Holy Spirit.

The baptism of Jesus also throws much helpful light upon the use of denials and affirmations. The denial, like water baptism, has to do with cleansing, or letting go. But the denial is not complete in itself. The denial does only preparatory work, and should always be followed by the corresponding affirmation—just as the water baptism of Jesus was followed by the descent of the Holy Spirit. Through denial we are cleansed; by affirmation we are infilled with the desired good.

It should be further noted that when Jesus thus dedicated himself to his God-given ministry, the dedication was followed not only by the descent of the Holy Spirit, but also by the message of divine approval. In like manner, as we dedicate ourselves to God's service and are ready and willing to follow his directions, we also become aware of divine approval; and once again is heard the message, "This is my beloved son, in whom I am well pleased"[79]

In order to understand fully the metaphysical meaning of this story of the baptism of Jesus, the following notes from *The Revealing Word*[80] should be carefully considered:

---

[79] Matthew 3:17
[80] Fillmore, Charles *The Revealing Word*, pp. 21, 22

"Baptism—the spiritual cleansing of the mind. Typifies the cleansing power and work of Spirit that redeems men from sin. It is the first step in the realization of Truth. When the baptizing power of the word is poured on a center in consciousness, it dissolves all material thought, and through this cleansing, purifying process, the individual is prepared to see and discern spiritually.
"The two baptisms, those of John and Jesus, represent the two common steps in spiritual development, denial and affirmation, or the dropping of the old and laying hold of the new. In the first baptism, that of John, through the power of the word, the sense man is erased from consciousness, and the mind is purged and made ready for the second baptism, that of Jesus. In the second baptism, the creative law of divine affirmation, set into action by supreme Mind, lights its fires at the center of man's being, and when thus kindled raises soul and body to a high degree of purity. This process is known as regeneration. ...

"Baptism, the Holy Spirit—A quickening of the spiritual nature that is reflected in mind and body. Spiritual baptism has power; it is affirmative; it is positive. This outpouring of the Holy Spirit is the second baptism. Christ represents this phase of baptism. It is the most precious gift of God and comes to those who steadfastly seek first the

kingdom of God and his righteousness. 'He shall
baptize you in the Holy Spirit'.[81]

Read the passages: Matthew 4:1-11; Mark 1:12-13; Luke
4:1-13

The Temptations

Note the following:

1. Mark makes only a general reference to this
    period of temptation.
2. Matthew and Luke give the complete story and
    are in essential agreement—except in the order
    of the temptations.
3. The period of time mentioned is "forty days."
    This may refer to an actual calendar period, or
    (as seems more likely) it may be an
    approximate statement, equivalent to our term
    "about a month." However, it is interesting and
    instructive to note how this word forty (days, or
    years) appears again and again in Scripture. In
    most instances the word forty indicates "a
    period of time necessary to complete the work
    that is being undertaken." "Forty days" would
    mean something like this in the story of the
    temptations of Jesus.

While reading the Scripture passages given above,
the questions will naturally arise: How should we think of
this period of temptation? What are the writers of these
stories actually seeking to convey to us? Several things
should be given careful consideration:

---

[81] Matthew 3:11

1. The word temptation, as here used, should not be thought of as meaning enticement to do wrong. Rather, the word should be regarded as indicating a time of testing, or proving; for it was through this testing or proving that Jesus was assured that he was really ready to enter upon his ministry. It will be noted that there are a number of references in the Bible where the "devil" is shown in the capacity of a "testing agent."[82]

2. The temptations as here recorded are more than unrelated incidents. Everything mentioned is clearly related to the forthcoming ministry of Jesus. The temptations represent what we may term the "pros and cons" of Jesus' thinking during this period. In other words, the temptations represent some of the challenges of the forthcoming ministry, such as had to be faced, and upon which decisions had to be made. Indeed, if we read the story of the temptations aright, we shall find that we are here actually thinking things through with Jesus.

Thus, a careful study of this period of temptation is important—because not only do we see Jesus coming through with flying colors (as the saying goes), but we are clearly shown how we also may become overcomers, as we face up to the various situations in life. Let us therefore consider these temptations of Jesus:

---

[82] See Job 1-2

First temptation[83]

At this time Jesus was not only physically hungry because of the period of fasting mentioned, but he was also facing an entirely new situation in life. Thus far Jesus had been a carpenter, and his daily bread had been earned through his work. He knew that if he did a certain job, the recompense therefrom would provide for his living. But now he was facing an entirely different situation. His work now was that of an itinerant preacher, and he would be called upon to go from place to place, traveling up and down the country. How could he be sure of his daily bread? True, God had endowed him with certain wonderful powers, and Jesus himself was aware of this; but was he justified in using these powers to provide for his own personal wants? Something within him said, "A man must live, you know!" But Jesus went deeper and found the right answer, as he said: "It is written, Man shall not live by bread alone, but by every word that proceeds out of the mouth of God".[84] It should be noted that Jesus' answer was almost a direct quotation from Deuteronomy 8:3.

Second and Third Temptations[85]

In order to understand the second and third temptations it is necessary to know something about what is usually termed "the Jewish messianic expectation." At the time of Jesus (and for many years prior to this) the Jewish people were looking for a heaven-sent deliverer, or

---

[83] Matthew 4:1-4
[84] Matthew 4:4
[85] Matthew 4:5-11

messiah (the Anointed One). It was believed that when this deliverer appeared, not only would he free the Jewish people from the Roman yoke, and overcome other enemies, but he would also re-establish the Jewish kingdom in a manner even exceeding the splendor and glories of the David-Solomon period. Many passages in Scripture encouraged the Jewish people to expect this deliverer; and at the time of Jesus the people were eagerly looking forward to the appearance of their messiah.

However, in this expectancy there was one important point of difference. People were asking: Just how, and in what form will this messiah appear? Some believed that a deliverer of this sort could come only in a supernatural way—a celestial being, descending to earth from the skies. A messiah of this type, people believed, could subdue the earth through fear, plus the exercise of his supernatural powers. However, others believed that the coming messiah would be of a warrior type— someone raised up in the midst of the nation, similar to David. They thought that a warrior of this sort would gather around him an army of patriots, strong enough to overthrow Rome, or any other arising world power. This warrior, or kingly type of messiah, is pictured in Psalms 72.

Now, with this background, the second and third temptations immediately take on new and important meaning. When Jesus was taken (either in thought, or in person) to the high pinnacle of the Temple, the thought came to him: "Cast thyself down ..." As he saw himself gradually descending into the Temple courts, upheld by the promised "angel hands",[86] he recognized that this

---

[86] See Psalms 91

would appear as a literal fulfillment of the Jewish expectancy, and all the people worshipping there would immediately acclaim him as the Messiah. Furthermore, all this would be in complete accord with the Scripture prediction: "And the Lord, whom ye seek, will suddenly come to his temple".[87] Thus, the second temptation resolved itself into a challenge to claim messiahship through a spectacular demonstration. The story indicates how all this was immediately rejected by Jesus.

Coming to the third temptation, it is not difficult to see that this is closely connected with the warrior, or kingly, type of messiah. The thought here is this: Just as the "kingdoms of the world" had been conquered by the armed might of Rome, so could Jesus and his army make conquest of the entire world, including Rome. In other words, the temptation was to gain a world kingdom by worldly means. Of course, Jesus also rejected this temptation—and how thorough and far-reaching was this rejection is indicated by the statement he made later: "My kingdom is not of this world: if my kingdom were of this world, then would my servants fight ... but now is my kingdom not from hence".[88]

In reading this story, it is most important for us to see just how Jesus overcame these temptations. This is not fully explained in the record, and checking in detail just how each temptation was met does not provide an explanation. Rather, we should look at the entire story to see if it contains some well-defined principles for overcoming, and which were used by Jesus at this time.

---

[87] Malachi 3:1
[88] John 18:36

Then, if these principles can be recognized and fully understood, we also shall be in a position to "go ... and do likewise."

These "overcoming principles" may be briefly outlined, as follows:

1. In meeting and overcoming these temptations, Jesus took the first step by putting God first. This applies in all three instances. The usual tendency is to put self first—to make personal provision, to receive personal acclaim, to gain personal power; but it will be noted that in each instance Jesus put God first.

2. Jesus then spoke a strong word of Truth, based on Scripture—and he shaped his statements to meet each arising challenge. It is both interesting and helpful to notice how Jesus used denials and affirmations in these statements.

3. Jesus then acted in accord with his spoken word. This is especially important—for it is through such actions that our statements become indeed "living words"!

Surely, we also can use these principles to meet and overcome every arising challenge or temptation in life.

Just at this point we may find ourselves inquiring: If Jesus thus rejected the current ideas regarding coming of the messiah, what actually was his attitude regarding the messiah? "What sort of messiah did Jesus visualize and seek to reveal? And how would such a messiah establish his kingdom?

We find the answers to these and similar questions in the teaching ministry of Jesus. This matter will be referred to again and again in these lessons.

At this time, therefore, it may be sufficient to say that as we read the Gospels it soon becomes clear that Jesus thought of the messiah, not as a glorified earthly monarch—one holding dominion over his subjects by fear and force—but rather as one who helped, inspired, and served his people. Jesus himself said, "I am in the midst of you as he that serves".[89] Further study reveals that Jesus saw himself as out-picturing the inspired poem of "the suffering servant".[90] This passage should be carefully read at this time.

Furthermore, Jesus saw the coming of the messiah, not as a spectacular, outer event, but rather as the reception of the Spirit of Truth into the hearts and lives of believers. He saw clearly that a messiahship established upon spectacular appearance or physical force would not endure; but a messiahship established through the reception of Truth, and maintained through loving service, would endure forever. Of course, this was not an entirely new viewpoint, originating with Jesus; several Hebrew writers sought to emphasize this spiritual-type messiah, but their words were, for the most part, overlooked until Jesus brought them to light. Refer back to Zechariah 9:9-10 and other similar passages. Several modern writers also have the same idea—as indicated in Phillips Brooks' Christmas Hymn:

---

[89] Luke 22:27
[90] Isaiah 52:13-53:12

"How silently, how silently, the wondrous gift is given! So God imparts to human hearts the blessings of his heaven. No ear may hear his coming, But in this world of sin, where meek souls will receive him still, the dear Christ enters in."[91]

---

[91] Unity Song Selections, 134

Chapter 4 - Jesus' Early Ministry

Historical Questions

1. Why did Jesus go to Cana in Galilee? (John 2:1-11) Explain briefly, in your own words, what happened at Cana.

2. What was taking place in the Temple courts when Jesus returned there at Passover time? (John 2:13-22) Explain briefly what action Jesus took at that time.

3. What attitude did the Temple officials take toward Jesus, following the above action? What was the basic cause of their hostility?

4. Who came to Jesus "by night"? Explain briefly the purpose of this visit, and tell how Jesus responded.

5. What very important teaching was given to Nicodemus at the close of the above interview? (John 3:16) Explain briefly what this teaching means to us today. Is this "eternal life" for some future time? Or may we experience it now?

Metaphysical Questions

1. Explain briefly the important metaphysical teaching given in Jesus' first miracle at Cana. (John 2:1-11) How does this apply to us today?

2. How would you interpret the story of the cleansing of the Temple? (John 2:13-22) How does this apply to us today?

3. Is there any special significance in the fact that this Temple cleansing is recorded in the Gospels as happening at different times? What would this mean in terms of present-day experience?

4. What does Nicodemus signify metaphysically? Explain fully. Also, what is indicated by the term "by night"?

5. What is the new birth? Discuss fully, and mention some steps we must take in order to enter into this experience.

Lesson Text

The Synoptic Gospels[92] indicate that Jesus began his ministry in Galilee. Indeed, Mark's Gospel, after telling briefly about the ministry of John the Baptizer, takes us immediately into Galilee, and gives us an account of the activities of Jesus in that area. However, John's Gospel tells us of some earlier happenings connected with the time when Jesus was doing some teaching work in and around Jerusalem. This period is often referred to as "the early Judean ministry."

Three outstanding events during this early period should be carefully considered:

Read the passage: John 2:1-11

The Wedding Feast at Cana.

At first sight it may appear somewhat strange to include a miracle performed in "Cana of Galilee" in the period designated "the early Judean ministry." Nevertheless, this miracle has a definite connection with

---

[92] Matthew, Mark and Luke

this period; so it will be well to give the story careful consideration.

Note the following:

1. At this time Jesus must have been engaged in his early teaching work in and around Jerusalem, as suggested above. The story tells how "Jesus also was bidden [to the wedding feast} and his disciples".[93] Jesus could scarcely have had "disciples" unless he was at that time fully established as a teacher.

2. The story further relates that "the mother of Jesus was [already] there".[94] This seems to indicate that there were ties of friendship, or distant relationship, between the family at Cana and the family at near-by Nazareth; and for this special occasion Mary had gone to Cana to assist in the preparations for the marriage feast. At this time Jesus was engaged in his "early Judean ministry," but a special invitation was sent to him, "requesting the honor of his company." It would be regarded as a great distinction to have this young Teacher whose fame was already widespread) present at the wedding feast.

3. At events of this sort, it was customary for the family to provide the "good things to eat"; but in many instances the guests brought the wine. The story tells how on this occasion, for some reason not disclosed, the wine ran short, and the entire feast was in danger of becoming a dismal failure.

---

[93] John 2:2
[94] John 2:1

Moreover, there would be "loss of face" for the families involved—and this would be indeed a tragedy of tragedies!

4. Note the use, by Jesus, of the word woman.[95] To the present-day reader this word may sound somewhat disrespectful. However, rightly understood, there is no disrespect here. Rather, this is what may be termed an impersonal form of address—much the same as if we would say, "My dear Madam." And, in this connection, it is significant to note that throughout his ministry, as recorded in the Gospels, Jesus did not speak of Mary as his mother.

5. Also, the phrase "mine hour is not yet come" should not be interpreted as an indication of the coming miracle. Rather, this should be regarded as referring to the custom of serving the wine according to the age of the providing guests—the wine given by the eldest guest being served first, and then in a similar manner right down the line. Jesus would have been regarded as a young man at that time, and consequently it would have been out of order for him to thrust himself forward until his "age bracket" had been reached. Later on, when the actual need was realized, and when the servants looked to Jesus for wine, he did not fail to provide what was needed.

How should we interpret this miracle? Two possibilities present themselves:

---

[95] John 2:4

1. We may direct our attention to the details given in the story; and in these we shall undoubtedly find many interesting and helpful suggestions.
2. However, the better plan is to look for the central, or really important, teaching in the miracle. As we give our attention to this, we shall find that the details will then fall into right relationship. All this will be further discussed in a later lesson.

For this miracle, then, let us follow the second plan suggested above, and try to see what is the really important teaching here. Note the following:

1. Just as a marriage indicates union between two persons, so we may recognize—in a metaphysical way—union between faculties, or states of consciousness. We may think of union between wisdom and love, or intellectual ideas and spiritual ideas, and so on; and such a union is usually associated with joyous experiences. We may also recognize the wine, as mentioned in the miracle, as a symbol of life, or life forces. And again, the free flow of life forces is usually associated with happiness, joy, and similar pleasurable experiences.
2. However, there are times when something happens—something which tends to mar all these joyous experiences. At the wedding, the supply of wine gave out. In life's experiences there are times when "the bottom drops out of things," and the outlook becomes very dismal indeed. What is to be done in such a situation? Is there any way of holding off the impending disaster? Yes, there is.

Note what was done at the wedding: The persons immediately concerned looked to Jesus—and he not only held off the "impending disaster" but also furnished a new and abundant supply of wine, and the quality thereof was far superior to anything the guests had tasted before. We may also recognize in this ample supply of superior wine (symbol of life) an interesting and helpful commentary on the statement used later by Jesus: "I came that they may have life, and may have it abundantly".[96] Thus, we may sum up the important teaching of this miracle in a brief sentence: If the joys of life should seem to be running low, call upon Jesus Christ, for he will always respond—and his response will be in a measure "exceeding abundantly above all that we ask or think".[97]

Read the passage: John 2:13-22

Cleansing the Temple

Following the wedding feast at Cana, and after a very brief stay at Capernaum, Jesus hastened back to Jerusalem, in order to be there for the Passover observances. However, after arriving at Jerusalem and attempting to take his former teaching-place in the Temple courts,[98] Jesus found the entire area occupied by

---

[96] John 10:10

[97] Ephesians 3:20

[98] Note: In this passage, and in many other places in the Christian Scriptures, we find reference to someone being either "in the Temple," or "going to the Temple." It should be understood here, and in all similar instances, that the word Temple actually indicates the Temple courts. Only the priests entered

money-changers and sellers of sacrificial animals. Hence, we have the story of the cleansing of the Temple, as given in the above Scripture passage.

As we look carefully into the story of cleansing the Temple, one important feature calls for immediate attention:

From the Scripture passage given above, it would appear that this cleansing took place during what we have termed "the early Judean ministry" of Jesus. In other words, this was one of Jesus' earlier activities. However, the Synoptic Gospels place the cleansing of the Temple almost at the close of Jesus' ministry—immediately following the triumphal entry, and just prior to' the Crucifixion.[99] This suggests two possibilities:

1. That there were two cleansings: The first, as recorded in John's Gospel, and the second as recorded in the Synoptic Gospels—and these separated by the period of Jesus' ministry.

2. That there was only one cleansing—at the time indicated by the synoptic writers. The writer of John's Gospel, recognizing the importance of this activity, and fearing that it might be overshadowed by the events just prior to the Crucifixion, placed it at the earlier period. All this seems quite possible; but at the same time it must be recognized that what was indicated in the first suggestion is also

---

the actual Temple building, while all other persons remained in the various courts surrounding the Temple. It is important to recognize this distinction—because nowadays, when we refer to someone "going to church," we mean actually entering the church building, and not merely waiting in the area surrounding the church.)

[99] See Matt. 21:12-17; Mark 11:15-18; Luke 19:45-48.

equally possible. However, the really essential thing is to recognize the great importance of this happening—and this importance is emphasized by the fact that the cleansing story is recorded in all four Gospels.

The question now arises: Why did Jesus do this? Just what was Jesus' purpose in this cleansing of the Temple?

Let us consider several possibilities:

1. Should we regard Jesus' action as a strong protest against what we might term "desecration of holy ground"? Was Jesus thus showing his disapproval of using the Temple courts for this sort of thing? In point of fact, this is the explanation usually given for the cleansing of the Temple. Jesus was not saying that the things mentioned might not have a rightful place somewhere; but he did emphasize that that "somewhere" was decidedly not in the vicinity of the Temple! Moreover, there are several indications that Jesus felt quite strongly on this subject. John 2:16 reads: "take these things hence; make not my Father's house a house of merchandise," while Mark 11:16 informs us that "he would not suffer that any man should carry a vessel through the temple [court]."

2. However, looking a little deeper into the story, there seems a possibility that Jesus was here doing something more than protesting against desecration. It may be that he was protesting against the very system which brought about the conditions he was witnessing at that time. True,

this sacrificial system dated back into antiquity, and many passages of the Hebrew Scriptures fully supported it. But Jesus must have recognized (as we now recognize) that such a system was little more than a relic of ancient idolatry and barbarity. In earlier days several Hebrew Scripture writers had registered their protests, but apparently all to no purpose. The idea of sacrificing something was so deeply embedded in the traditional forms of worship that all suggestions of reform were frowned upon. Moreover, this sacrificial system was so profitable to the priests and all others immediately concerned that they were determined to maintain it at all costs. Perhaps it was this, more than anything else, that aroused the hostility of the Sadducees and others associated with the Temple against Jesus. They feared that Jesus was seeking to undermine their traditions, prestige, and income; and therefore they must do away with him!

3. Most important of all, we should recognize that Jesus was here seeking to impart to us a truly outstanding lesson. This lesson is emphasized in the latter part of the story, where we read the Gospel writer's comment: "But he spoke of the temple of his body".[100] We also should recognize the need for cleansing our body temple — for:[101]

---

[100] John 2:21
[101] Fillmore, Charles *Mysteries of John*, p. 28

"When we throw the light of Spirit into the subconscious courts of the body temple, we find queer and often startling conditions there. One would hardly expect to see butcher stalls and money changers in a temple built for the worship of God, yet similar conditions exist in all of us".

The following indicates how this cleansing is to be accomplished:

"So the body temple must be cleansed; it is the house of God ('for we are a temple of the living God'), and it should be put in order. The first step in this cleansing process is to recognize its need. The next step is the 'scourge of small cords'[102] to formulate the word or statement of denial. When we deny in general terms we cleanse the consciousness, but secret sins may yet lurk in the inner parts. The words that most easily reach these hidden errors are not great ones, such as 'I am one with Almightiness; my environment is God' but small, definite statements that cut like whipcords into the sensuous fleshly mentality.

"To get perfect results it is necessary to deal with our mind in both the absolute and the relative. In the early morning we may affirm, 'All the affairs of my life are under the law of justice, and my own comes to me in ways divine,' and before noon we find ourselves searching the papers for advertisements of bargains in the stores. Such an experience shows that we have not gone into the

---

[102] King James Version

temple and tipped over the tables and scattered the coins".[103]

As we thus go to work on cleansing our body temple, there may be revealed to us the reason for this apparent duplication of this story in the Gospel records, as discussed earlier in this lesson. In actual experience we often find that one cleansing is not sufficient, and that the cleansing process must be repeated. We may cleanse our temple at the beginning of our daily activities, just as Jesus did at the beginning of his ministry; but some more cleansing has to be done later on, just as Jesus did at the close of his ministry.

Read the passage: John 3

Visit of Nicodemus

If we would really understand this third chapter of John, we should first do a little reconstruction work.

Look carefully at John 3:3, and note how the verse reads: "Jesus answered and said unto him ..." Now the word answered would seem to indicate that a question had been asked, a request made, or something similar. But as we look back at the preceding verse we find that no question had been asked. Nicodemus simply greeted Jesus in the somewhat elaborate Eastern manner—but nothing further is indicated. Yet the question (for indeed there must have been a question) is actually the key to the entire discourse that follows.

What, then, was the question? Why does it not appear in the text?

---

[103] Ibid, p. 29

Answering the second inquiry first: There is a possibility that John deliberately omitted the question for reasons known to himself, and which we shall not attempt to discuss here. More likely, however, the question was accidentally omitted by a copyist in the early hand-written days of the Scriptures, and somehow the error was not rectified.

However, the really important point is the substance of the question itself; and fortunately, Jesus' answer gives us a most helpful clue. Note how Jesus mentions here "the kingdom of God"[104] — and in this connection we recall that in Jesus' early ministry he frequently spoke of "the kingdom."[105] Moreover, the Jewish people at that time would naturally associate this "kingdom" with the "messianic expectancy," as discussed in an earlier lesson. Thus, while it may not be possible to give the exact wording, we can reconstruct the substance of Nicodemus' question, somewhat as follows (perhaps it will be best to give the preceding and following verses, so that the actual question will fit naturally in its place):

> "Now there was a man of the Pharisees, named Nicodemus, a ruler of the Jews: the same came unto him by night, and said to him, Rabbi, we know that thou art a teacher come from God; for no one can do these signs that thou do, except God be with him." Nicodemus then went on to say: "Rabbi, we have often heard thee speak of 'the kingdom'—and this is a very vital subject with us. Tell us, therefore,

---

[104] John 3:3
[105] See Mark 1:15

more about this kingdom. When will this kingdom come? In what manner will it be established? And what must we do to obtain our rightful place in this kingdom?" "Jesus answered and said unto him, Verily, verily, I say unto thee, except one be born anew, he cannot [even] see the kingdom of God."

With the passage thus set clearly before us, we are able to see new meaning and purpose in Jesus' statement regarding being "born anew." Jesus was here telling Nicodemus that these inquiries regarding the kingdom were all to no purpose. This was a spiritual kingdom, and could be comprehended only by those who were spiritually quickened. Thus, to be "born anew" was the only way to "see the kingdom of God."

Several points in this chapter call for special attention:

The New Birth

Jesus told Nicodemus "Ye must be born anew"[106] The Authorized Version states "again," while the marginal reading is "from above" —and this latter is perhaps the most helpful reading. What is this "new birth"? What does it indicate in our experience?

Perhaps the simplest way is to recognize that we may think of ourselves in terms of "physical," "mental," and "spiritual." As we begin our life experience we are born physically; this is a physical birth, and we are then a physical being. Later comes the mental, or intellectual awakening; and then, in addition to the physical, we are an

---

[106] John 3:7

intellectual being. Finally, there comes the spiritual awakening, and we are "born from above"—a spiritual being. The word birth as here used should be regarded as including both the quickening and the coming forth into activity and manifestation.

However, there is a difference between the earlier processes mentioned—physical and intellectual—and the spiritual awakening. The physical and intellectual processes happen, as we say, naturally; but the spiritual awakening—in accord with our freedom of choice—comes only as the result of our earnest desire. The spiritual birth is not forced upon us, but must be sought and gained. True, there is always the spiritual potentiality within us; but for the actual awakening and coming forth into manifestation, we ourselves must take the initiative.

The following quotations will also help toward an understanding of the subject:[107]

> "New Birth—the realization by us of our identity, with the fullness of power and glory that follows.
>
> "A birth is a coming into a state of being. Man first is born, or comes into a state of physical being; he thinks of himself as flesh, material. The 'new birth' is the coming into a higher state of being that is alive to the fact that man is like God, one with God"

In John 3:5 Jesus speaks of being "born of water and the Spirit." This may be explained as follows: [108]

---

[107] Fillmore, Charles *The Revealing Word*, p. 140
[108] *Metaphysical Bible Dictionary*, pp. 482-83 - Nicodemus

To be 'born of water' is to be cleansed of all impurity, sin, and materiality, through denial. To be 'born of the Spirit' is to come into the consciousness of divine law and to lift the whole man into a new life of harmony and order by affirmative prayer.

Nicodemus

Thinking in terms of Nicodemus himself, the following should be carefully noted:

John's Gospel states that Nicodemus came to Jesus "by night." Undoubtedly, Nicodemus had listened to the teaching of Jesus in the Temple courts during the day, and could have asked questions then. Apparently he did not. Could it be, therefore, that Nicodemus hesitated to identify himself openly with this new teaching because he feared public opinion? It should be remembered here that Nicodemus was a well-known public official, wealthy, and a member of the Sanhedrin. The coming "by night" seems to indicate that Nicodemus was afraid of something. Also, it would seem that the writer of John's Gospel was not favorably impressed with Nicodemus' behavior; for not only does he mention this coming "by night" here, but also in a later story he mentions "Nicodemus, he who at the first came to him [Jesus] by night".[109]

What does all this mean to us? The following passages contain some very important teaching:

"Nicodemus' coming to Jesus (spiritual I AM) 'by night' (spiritual darkness) shows that intellectual learning counts for naught in the regeneration. Man must be born

---

[109] John 19:39

of Spirit in order to be redeemed. ... The ruling tendency of our surface religion is spiritual darkness; so it is represented as coming to Jesus (spiritual I AM) by night. But there is that in it which is pure (pure blood), is single in its desire to know Truth, and is seeking the light; when we begin to ask the cause of the works of healing that are being done on every hand by people who believe in Truth, we are acknowledging that there is evidence of divine power".[110]

Perhaps Jesus was giving emphasis to ideas similar to those indicated above, when he said to Nicodemus:

> *"And this is the judgment, that the light is come into the world, and men loved the darkness rather than the light; for their works were evil. For every one that doeth evil hates the light, lest his works should be reproved. But he that doeth the truth cometh to the light that his works may be made manifest, that they have been wrought in God".[111]*

Yet, notwithstanding all the fears and shortcomings of Nicodemus, Jesus must have seen in him something really worthwhile. Note the length of the discourse, and the many important statements contained therein. Note also how Jesus at that time gave to Nicodemus the priceless statement which has since come to be regarded as representing the very heart of Christian teaching:[112]

---

[110] *Metaphysical Bible Dictionary*, p. 482
[111] John 3:19-21
[112] John 3:16

For God so loved the world, that he gave his only begotten son, that whosoever believeth on him should not perish, but have eternal life.

Chapter 5 - Jesus Makes an Important Decision

Historical Questions

1. Why did Jesus transfer his activities from Jerusalem to Galilee? (John 4:1-3) Indicate several possible reasons for this change of locale, giving Scripture references.

2. Using your own words, briefly tell the story of Jesus and the woman at the well. (John 4:4-42) Be sure to include two important statements given by Jesus at this time.

3. Briefly explain the statement, "For Jews have no dealings with Samaritans." (John 4:9) What was the attitude of Jesus in this regard?

4. Why did Jesus gather around him a group of twelve disciples? Suggest two or three practical reasons for this procedure.

5. Tell briefly, using your own words, the story of the healing at Cana-Capernaum. (John 4:46-54)

Metaphysical Questions

1. Explain briefly why, in our spiritual development, we leave "Judea" and go into "Galilee." What do these places represent in our consciousness?

2. What does the woman at the well represent in our experience? (John 4:4-42) Explain why it is that after drinking of "this water" we "thirst again." Where is true satisfaction to be found?

3. How would you explain the statement, "God is Spirit"? (John 4:24) Also explain briefly how we may "worship the Father in spirit and truth." (John 4:19-23)

4. What do the twelve disciples represent in our consciousness? Give the metaphysical meaning of each name.

5. Read carefully the story of the healing at Cana-Capernaum (John 4:46-54), and then:

   (a) explain how faith helped in this healing;

   (b) explain briefly what is indicated by the term "absent treatment."

Lesson Text

Read the passage: John 4:1-3

Departure from Judea.

When reading the above passage we may get the impression that this is merely a casual reference to another brief visit to Galilee, such as Jesus had recently made. Or we may think that possibly there was some "unfinished business" in Galilee that needed Jesus' attention. Actually, however, we are here reading about a momentous decision on the part of Jesus, a decision which not only altered the course of his ministry, but also in all probability prolonged his activity for nearly two years. Moreover, because of this decision, we now have the record of some very important happenings, some outstanding teaching, and also some very practical lessons which are just as applicable today as they were at the time of Jesus' ministry. So let us look carefully at the situation here presented.

Until this time Jesus had been conducting a teaching ministry in and around Jerusalem. In all probability Jesus taught regularly in the Temple courts, as did other teachers in those days. From time to time some of Jesus' listeners would ask for baptism; a baptismal service would be arranged, with the actual baptism taking place in one of the tributaries of the river Jordan, a little distance outside Jerusalem. These ceremonies would be similar to those held by John the Baptizer, who was still conducting his ministry. However, it should be noted that Jesus deputized some of his disciples to perform the actual work of baptizing.[113] And it would seem that at this time the popularity of Jesus' teaching was increasing, for the candidates for his baptism were numbering more than those seeking baptism from John the Baptizer.

Why, then, did Jesus decide to leave this rapidly developing ministry in and around Jerusalem, and depart into Galilee? It is clear that this was no "snap decision," arising out of some trivial incident. There must have been some deep-seated causes for Jesus' action; and it is possible for us to trace some of these causes.

1. Scripture indicates that by this time the ministries of Jesus and John the Baptizer had become (to use a modern word) competitive; and it is clear that such was contrary to the wishes of Jesus.[114] Furthermore, this competition was engendering controversy and

---

[113] See John 4:2
[114] John 4:1

ill-feeling; and Jesus had no desire that his followers should spend time quibbling over details. It may also have been that Jesus recognized that the time had come for a complete break with John the Baptizer and his teachings—for, as Jesus put it, "No one puts new wine into old wine-skins".[115]

2. In seeking possible causes for Jesus' departure into Galilee, we should recall that shortly after this time John the Baptizer was arrested, imprisoned, and put to death. John's political activities and denunciations aroused Herod's anger, and the Baptizer's ministry was brought to an untimely end. May it be, therefore, that Jesus foresaw these happenings and sought to forestall the possibility of a second tragedy by carrying his ministry into a region beyond the jurisdiction of Herod? Such action should not be regarded as an indication that Jesus feared Herod, or any activity of Herod. Rather, the indication is that Jesus had planned an extended ministry, and was taking all necessary steps to insure its continuity and completion. So far from Jesus fearing death or imprisonment, he stated clearly: "No man taketh it [my life} away from me ... I have power to lay it down, and I have power to take it again".[116] It is well to note that after completing his Galilean activities, Jesus

---

[115] Mark 2:18-22
[116] John 10:18

returned to Jerusalem to face far graver dangers than those arising from the displeasure of Herod.

3. Something which must have concerned Jesus deeply is indicated in the visit of Nicodemus.[117] Rereading this story, as it applies to our present discussion, we recognize that when Jesus was teaching in Jerusalem he was dealing mainly with people who were deeply entrenched in the old, traditional religious beliefs. The religious leaders in Jerusalem were quite satisfied with the teaching and interpretation they already had. While some of them acted in a patronizing manner toward this new Teacher, they had no intention of accepting the teaching he was presenting. Nicodemus' coming to Jesus "by night" indicated clearly the general attitude of the religious leaders. Jesus therefore decided to move to a more promising area, which, while not exactly virgin soil, might prove more open and receptive to his teachings.

So there may have been several reasons why Jesus "left Judea and departed again into Galilee." But it will be noted that all these had to do with what might be termed external conditions. As we look deeper into the matter, it is possible to discern here a very important metaphysical lesson. Consider the following suggestions:

The words Judea and Judah have as their root meaning "Praise of Jehovah".[118] Also, Jesus spoke of the

---

[117] See John 3:1-21
[118] *Metaphysical Bible Dictionary*, p 372

Temple at Jerusalem as "a house of prayer".[119] Thus Judea and Jerusalem are closely associated with the idea of praise and prayer. But should we regard praise and prayer as an end in itself? Scarcely! The spiritual blessings coming to us through praise and prayer should be carried out into all our daily activities. It is therefore both interesting and helpful to note that the word Galilee, metaphysically understood, indicates "energy of life; life activity".[120] Thus, while we recognize the necessity of spending some time in "Judea and Jerusalem" (praise and prayer), we must then "depart into Galilee" (life activity), where the inspiration, strength, and other blessings we have received may be translated into helpful activity. The following comment on the word Galilee may prove informative here:

"Jesus came into Galilee, and the Galileans received him. Spiritually interpreted, this means that the indwelling Christ reaches spiritual consummation ... in the measure that it manifests life and functions in Spirit consciousness".[121]

Read the passage: John 4:4-42

Journey through Samaria.
Verse 4: "he must needs pass through Samaria."
At this point, look at a map of the Holy Land [one showing the geographical divisions at the time of Jesus], and check the relative positions of Judea, Samaria, and Galilee. You will then see that a traveler, journeying

---

[119] Matthew 21:13
[120] *Metaphysical Bible Dictionary*, p. 222
[121] Fillmore, Charles *Mysteries of John*, p. 52

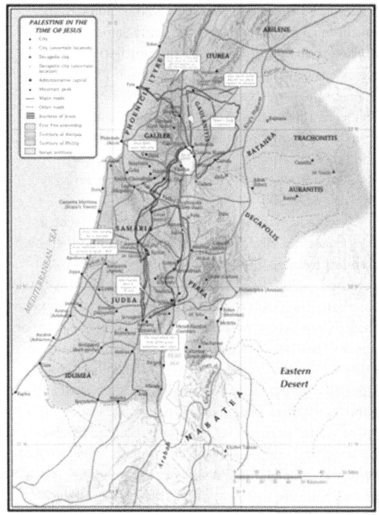

PALESTINE IN THE TIME OF JESUS

northward from Judea to Galilee, "must needs pass through Samaria"—for this would be the direct route. Why, then, does the writer of John's Gospel call special attention to this?

The Samaria of Jesus' time formed part of what was earlier known as the Northern Kingdom of Israel. This separate kingdom was set up following the death of King

Solomon.[122] The city of Samaria was the capital of this northern kingdom, and later the name Samaria was also applied to the entire province. This northern kingdom of Israel was overthrown by the Assyrians in 722 BCE, and many of the Israelites were carried away to Assyria. Following this, the Assyrians sent groups of poor people from that country into the overthrown kingdom of Israel; and these, intermarrying with the remaining poor Israelites, produced the mixed race later known as Samaritans.[123]

The Samaritans claimed Abraham and Jacob as their ancestors. Also, while the Samaritans had their own forms of worship, they held to the laws of Moses, and regarded the Books of Moses (Genesis, Exodus, Leviticus, Numbers, and Deuteronomy) as their scriptures. However, they did not accept as scripture the Books of the Prophets, nor the later books now found in the Old Testament. In other words, the "religious clock" of the Samaritans stopped with the fall of Samaria in 722 BCE. On the other hand, the Judean Jews placed great emphasis upon the "pure blood" of their race, and they accepted as scripture not only "the Law," but also "the Prophets" and the "Holy Writings." Indeed, the Judean Jews regarded themselves as the "spiritual aristocracy," and they despised the Samaritans.

Thus, when the writer of John's Gospel states that "He [Jesus] must needs pass through Samaria," this may have been in the nature of a rebuke against this race prejudice. In any case, there are indications in the

---

[122] See I Kings 12
[123] See II Kings 17:

Scriptures that Jesus had a deep regard for these despised Samaritans. For example, note the parable of the Good Samaritan[124] and several other instances. Jesus also recognized the needs of the Samaritans; and although there is no record of an extended ministry in this area, his one visit made a great contribution, both to the Samaritans and to Christianity as a whole.

Verse 6: "It was about the sixth hour."

At the time of Jesus, the Jewish people reckoned the day as a period of twelve hours, starting at six o'clock in the morning and lasting until six o'clock in the evening. Thus, the "sixth hour" would indicate the period corresponding to our noontime.

The question arises: Why would this woman come to the well to draw water during the hottest period of the day—at noon? Water was usually drawn during the cool period of early morning, or at sundown. Noontime, with the scorching sun overhead, would seem to be the most undesirable time to draw water! The explanation is to be found in the woman herself. Later in the chapter[125] there are indications that the woman's morals were not of the highest order; and consequently she was often slighted or shunned by the other women of the village when they met at this water-drawing point. Hence, on this occasion, she had come to the well hoping that nobody would be around, and she would be spared the insults and cruel behavior of her neighbors. Her chagrin in finding

---

[124] Luke 10:25-37
[125] Verses 17-18

somebody at the well is reflected in her reply to Jesus, when he asked her for a drink of water.

In verse 24: Many translations read, "God is Spirit," rather than "God is a Spirit". The reading "God is Spirit" is more satisfactory, since "a Spirit" might indicate the possibility of other Spirits—and this, we feel, would be far from the meaning of Jesus' words! However, the really important emphasis in this section is upon the idea of God's omnipresence. The worship of God is not to be limited to certain localities. Some persons may claim, "Only in Jerusalem," while others declare, "only in Samaria," or some other place. But in the teaching of Jesus we are assured that wherever we are, or whatever may be the circumstances, we may contact God. The only requirement is that we must worship God "in spirit and truth"; and we are assured that "such doth the Father seek to be his worshippers."

Reading this entire passage from a metaphysical viewpoint, we readily recognize the woman at the well as representing that deep-seated longing within human consciousness for something that will really satisfy. There are some things in life that offer temporary satisfaction; but these are not sufficient. When this temporary satisfaction is past, we still find ourselves thirsting, hungering, and longing for something that will really meet our need. Jesus recognized all this when he said to the woman, "Every one that drinks of this water shall thirst again".[126] We know from experience that one journey to the well is not sufficient. We find ourselves going back

---

[126] John 4:13

there time after time; and even then, at the end of all our journeys, we still "thirst again."

But at this point we may ask: Why should such a condition prevail? Why is it that we are unable to obtain the satisfaction we seek? The answer is right at hand: We are spiritual beings, and only that which is spiritual has power to fully satisfy our needs. We may find temporary satisfaction in physical things; but that which is spiritual in us cries out for its spiritual counterpart. Physical food may meet the needs of our physical nature, but the spiritual nature calls out for spiritual sustenance. Hence, we find Jesus saying: "Whosoever drinks of the water that I shall give him shall never thirst; but the water that I shall give him shall become in him a well of water springing up unto eternal life".[127] This teaching is beautifully expressed in a well-known hymn:

> "I heard the voice of Jesus say, 'Behold, I freely give the living water, thirsty one, Stoop down, and drink, and live:' I came to Jesus, and I drank of that life-giving stream; My thirst was quenched, my soul revived, and now I live in him."

Read the passages: Matthew 4:18-22; Matthew 9:9-13; Matthew 10:1-4; Mark 1:14-20; Luke 5:27-32; Luke 6:12-17

Choosing the Twelve

At first reading the above passages may appear to be in conflict with the account of the early followers of

---

[127] John 4:14

Jesus, as given in John 1:35-51.[128] This account tells of six disciples coming to Jesus during the ministry of John the Baptizer; while the synoptic accounts (given above) seem to indicate that Jesus called his disciples when he was opening up the Galilean ministry. However, the explanation may be found in the fact that Jesus, during his early Judean ministry, gathered around him what we may term a preliminary group of disciples. At that time these disciples had not given up their regular occupations, but were closely attending upon the ministry of Jesus in and around Jerusalem. Later on, however, when Jesus began his Galilean ministry, he organized the group of twelve full-fledged disciples, which included the former six; and all the disciples then abandoned their former occupations, and devoted their whole time to becoming "fishers of men."

At this point in our study, a twofold question presents itself, and calls for consideration: What was the purpose of Jesus in organizing this group of disciples? Why did he decide to make it a group of twelve?

Several possibilities should be recognized:

1. A regularly organized group such as this would provide protection and companionship for the Teacher; and this was something very needful during the Galilean ministry.
2. This group would be regarded as what we might term "teachers in training." Not only did they hear all the general lessons given by Jesus, but he also gave them special instructions and

---

[128] Refer back to chapter 2

explanations.[129] These disciples also took part in baptismal and similar services,[130] and they were later sent forth on special preaching missions (see Matt. 10). In a word, the disciples were organized to extend and continue the ministry of Jesus.

3. The number twelve would have special significance for the Jewish people of those times. Twelve would remind them of the twelve tribes of Israel, the component parts of the nation as a whole. This would also be an indication of the inclusiveness of Jesus' ministry, and would emphasize the fact that his purpose was to re-gather the "lost sheep of the house of Israel".[131] Then there would be the suggestion, in symbolic form, of the formation of the New Israel, or "the Kingdom," so often referred to by Jesus.

4. Going a step further, we may discern here a very important spiritual lesson—a pattern for us to follow, if we would develop our spiritual consciousness. The twelve disciples may be regarded as symbols of our twelve spiritual powers; and just as Jesus called, instructed, and sent forth his disciples, so we must deal likewise with our spiritual powers. What Jesus did, we also must do, if we would attain spiritual maturity. All this is fully discussed and

---

[129] See Mark 4:10-20
[130] See John 4:2
[131] See Matthew 15:24

explained in the book *The Twelve Powers of Man*, by Charles Fillmore.

At this time we should become familiar with two words used to designate this group of Jesus' followers. In Biblical usage they are sometimes called "disciples"; and this word indicates their position as students, or learners, in close fellowship with the teacher. But in other instances they are referred to as "apostles"; and this word means "those sent forth," usually to accomplish some special mission. The Scriptures make it clear that the special mission of the apostles was to teach the people 4hey contacted about those things in which the apostles themselves had been instructed while they were disciples.

The names of the twelve disciples (or apostles) of Jesus, together with what they symbolize in consciousness, may now be listed as follows:

1. Peter (Simon, Cephas): Faith.
2. Andrew (brother of Peter): Strength.
3. James (son of Zebedee): Wisdom, or Discriminating Judgment.
4. John (brother of James): Love.
5. Philip: Power.
6. Bartholomew (or Nathanael): Imagination.
7. Thomas: Understanding, or Spiritual Illumination.
8. Matthew (or Levi): Will.
9. James (The Less, son of Alphaeus): Divine Order.
10. Thaddaeus: Renunciation.
11. Simon (The Zealot, or Cananasan): Zeal, Enthusiasm.
12. Judas Iscariot: Life powers as yet unredeemed.

Read the passage: John 4:46-54

Healing at Cana-Capernaum

We should now look at the map of the Holy Land, and carefully check the geographical positions of Cana and Capernaum.

The above passage indicates that Jesus, in entering upon his Galilean ministry, made another visit to Cana, where some time earlier he had attended the wedding feast.[132] The nobleman mentioned in this passage lived at Capernaum, some twenty miles distant, and he had a son who was seriously sick. Hence, the nobleman hastened to Cana, intending to bring Jesus back to Capernaum, so that the sick son might receive healing treatment. All this seems quite clear.

But the conversation between Jesus and the nobleman, as here reported, needs careful consideration. Actually, the words of Jesus seem to be in the nature of a rebuke. Speaking to the nobleman, Jesus is reported to have said: "Except ye see signs and wonders, ye will in no wise believe".[133] But there is no indication in this passage that the nobleman had expressed any doubts regarding the power of Jesus. On the contrary, the nobleman's hurried journey from Capernaum to Cana might well be regarded as an indication of his wholehearted faith in Jesus' power to heal. It is quite possible that the nobleman had thought healing could come about only through a personal visit by Jesus to Capernaum, with the

---

[132] John 2:1-11
[133] John 4:48

accompanying laying on of hands or repetition of some magical formula; but all this could scarcely be regarded as unbelief.

The suggestion is therefore made that, for purposes of clarification, and as a help to our study, we should think of the above-mentioned conversation taking place somewhat as follows:

First, we should recall that the conversation took place at Cana, and people there were still talking about the miracle that Jesus had performed at the wedding feast some time earlier. Therefore, when the nobleman arrived, he may have said to Jesus: "Please come quickly with me to Capernaum, and heal my son. Just as you performed a miracle here at the wedding feast, will you now perform another miracle for my suffering son? Please come with me right away!"

However, Jesus recognized that Capernaum was many miles away, and much precious time would be consumed by the journey. Furthermore, the son's illness had now reached a critical stage, and delay might prove disastrous. Jesus thereupon said (in so many words) to the nobleman: "Can you believe without seeing signs and wonders? Or, in other words, have you faith enough to believe that your son can be healed without our journeying to Capernaum?" To which the nobleman might have replied, "Lord, I believe that all things are possible with Thee!" Jesus then said: "Go thy way; thy son live." And John records that "The man believed the word that Jesus spoke unto him, and ... his son lived."

Reading the story in this way, the details seem to fit together in an orderly pattern, and we are better able to understand the sequel, as given below.

However, before we come to this sequel, two other points should be briefly considered:

Meaning of Names

Cana: "Cana of Galilee [symbolizes} ... the power center in consciousness".[134]

Capernaum: "Capernaum (village of consolation, shelter of comfort, covering of compassion) refers to an inner conviction of the abiding compassion and restoring power of being. When one enters this state of consciousness a healing virtue pours out of the soul and transforms all discord to harmony".[135]

This story places emphasis upon what we sometimes term "absent treatment." The healing word was spoken in Cana (place of power), but its effect was felt in Capernaum (symbol of comfort, consolation, compassion). The power of the spoken word is not limited by time or space, as the Psalmist reminds us: "he sends his word, and heals them".[136] The following comments on "absent treatment" will prove helpful:

"The light of Truth is shining more brightly today than ever before. The same faith that healed the nobleman's son will heal all persons who open their minds to it and let go of prejudice and unbelief. This fact is being demonstrated to all who are willing to believe.

---

[134] *Metaphysical Bible Dictionary* p. 138
[135] *Ibid*, p. 139
[136] Psalms 107:20

"Faith on the part of the patient or of someone connected with him is found to be an important factor in absent healing. This nobleman had faith that Jesus could heal his son, and when Jesus uttered the positive truth 'Go thy way; thy son lives,' he 'believed the word' . . .

"When the word goes forth from a spiritual center (represented by Jesus and his apostles) it becomes a continuous life-giver to all who believe in the spiritual as the source of life. Through faith they 'tune in' and catch the message from the living word. 'The words that I have spoken unto you are spirit, and are life.' 'Heaven and earth shall pass away: but my words shall not pass away' ".[137]

Now for the sequel mentioned above: There is an old legend which tells how this nobleman, to show his gratitude for the healing of his son, placed his house at the disposal of Jesus, when the Master later came to Capernaum. The Scriptures indicate that Jesus made Capernaum the central point in his Galilean ministry; and there are several references to Jesus' using a house such as that of the nobleman for his headquarters while operating in Capernaum and the surrounding territory. Gratitude was thus expressed, not only in word, but also by deed.

---

[137] Fillmore, Charles *Mysteries of John* pp. 54-55

Chapter 6 - The Teaching Ministry of Jesus (Part One)

Historical Questions

1. How is the kingdom message of Jesus stated in the first chapter of Mark's Gospel? How does this differ from a similar statement made earlier by John the Baptizer? (Matt. 3:2)

2. What is a precept? Explain briefly. List five helpful precepts given by Jesus in the Sermon on the Mount. Give chapter and verse references with each precept.

3. What is a parable? Give, briefly, three reasons why Jesus taught in parables.

4. Using your own words, tell in brief form the story of the Prodigal Son. (Luke 15:11-32)

5. Briefly explain the important lesson contained in the parable of the Talents. (Matt. 25:14-30)

Metaphysical Questions

1. Give a brief explanation of the term, "the kingdom of heaven." Where is this kingdom located?

2. What is indicated by the word repent? Is this a requirement for entrance into the kingdom?

3. Explain briefly. Explain briefly how the parable of the Sower emphasizes the importance of receptivity. (Matt. 13:1-9) What is the result, or reward, of good receptivity? What happens when there is lack of receptivity?

4. Read carefully the parable of the Two Sons (Matt. 21:28-32), and then state briefly what each of these sons represents in our consciousness.

5. What is the theme of Jesus' parable of the Wise and Foolish Virgins? How can we apply this theme to our everyday living?

Lesson Text
Read the passage: Matthew 5, 6, 7.

The Gospels contain many references to the teaching activities of Jesus. We are told how he taught in the Temple courts, in synagogues, by the lakeside, and wherever people gathered around him. The Gospels also preserve for us much of the material used by Jesus in his teaching. And in this connection it is interesting to note how Luke summarizes his Gospel, by referring to it as a "treatise ... concerning all that Jesus began to ... teach".[138] Furthermore, the Gospels place emphasis on the high order of Jesus' teaching, and its effect upon those who heard him. Note how Nicodemus is reported as saying, "Rabbi, we know that thou art a teacher come from God".[139] Also, the Sermon on the Mount closes with this significant footnote: "The multitudes were astonished at his teaching: for he taught them as one having authority, and not as their scribes".[140]

This lesson, therefore, will be devoted to what is often termed "the teaching ministry of Jesus."

---

[138] Acts: 1:1
[139] John 3:2
[140] Matthew 7:28-29

Two important phases of this teaching ministry should be given careful consideration:

Read the passage: Mark 1:14-15.

The Message of Jesus.

When glancing at those sections of the Gospels which deal with the teaching ministry of Jesus, the reader cannot help noticing how often the word kingdom occurs. This amounts to far more than a number of casual references, for again and again the word is given special emphasis. Jesus began his Galilean ministry by proclaiming, "The kingdom of God is at hand".[141] The Sermon on the Mount begins, "Blessed are the poor in spirit: for theirs is the kingdom of heaven".[142] Jesus taught us to pray, "Thy kingdom come".[143] Many of the parables of Jesus begin, "The kingdom of heaven is likened unto..."[144] Even when facing the Cross, Jesus said, "My kingdom is not of this world".[145] Many other references will come readily to mind.

From the above it will be seen that, while during his ministry Jesus spoke of many things, his main emphasis was upon "the kingdom." Indeed, it can be said that the message of Jesus was, in reality, the message of the kingdom. Seek a thorough understanding of this message, and what is actually indicated by the term "the kingdom"; to those who earnestly seek this understanding there is the promise: "For thus shall be richly supplied unto you

---

[141] Mark 1:15
[142] Matthew 5:3
[143] Matthew 6:10
[144] Matthew 13:24
[145] John 18:36

the entrance into the eternal kingdom of our Lord and Savior Jesus, the Christ".[146]

But at this point we may find oneself inquiring: "How are we to understand Jesus' kingdom message? What is the nature of this kingdom? Where is this kingdom located? How do we attain entrance into this kingdom?"

Such questions as these cannot be dealt with in any easy, offhand manner. We are not dealing here with a material kingdom, having geographical location and governed by earthly laws. Our concern is with a spiritual kingdom or state of consciousness, and "we must seek to interpret what is spiritual in spiritual language".[147] Jesus recognized all this, and he did not attempt to describe the kingdom in physical terms. Instead, he said, "The kingdom of heaven is like unto ...",[148] and similar statements. We can assume that he hoped through these suggestions to create in his hearers a spiritual quickening, with the accompanying spiritual perception of the kingdom.

However, Jesus did make several important statements regarding the kingdom, and these should be given careful consideration. Note the following:

Jesus assured us that the kingdom is "at hand."

In order to understand this, we must remember that for many years prior to the coming of Jesus Christ, the Jewish people had been expecting the Messiah and the setting up of his kingdom. But this expectancy was always projected into the distant future. It was a "hope long

---

[146] II Peter 1:11
[147] I Corinthians 2:13 Moffatt
[148] Matthew 13:31

deferred"! True, John the Baptizer proclaimed: "The kingdom of heaven is at hand";[149] but the context makes clear that he meant that the kingdom was imminent, or coming in the near future. With Jesus, however, the phrase "at hand" indicated that the kingdom had actually arrived. For him, the kingdom was not something to be anxiously awaited, but was literally "at hand." This is made clear in the following passage:

"And being asked by the Pharisees, when the kingdom of God cometh, he [Jesus] answered them and said, the kingdom of God cometh not with observation: neither shall they say, Lo, here! Or, There! For lo, the kingdom of God is within you" or, "in the midst of you".[150]

Jesus taught that the coming of the kingdom meant the attainment of our highest good.

A mention has already been made of the Messianic expectancy, which included the coming of the Messiah and the setting up of his kingdom. However, it must be recognized that this expectancy was accompanied by a great deal of fear and dread. This is made clear by Peter's quotation from the Book of Joel on the day of Pentecost.[151] Here the coming of the kingdom is referred to as "the great and terrible day of Jehovah".[152] John the Baptizer also proclaimed the coming of the kingdom in similar terms, saying, "He will gather his wheat into the

---

[149] Matthew 3:2
[150] Luke 17:20-21
[151] See Acts 2:14-21
[152] Joel 2:31

garner, but the chaff he will burn up with unquenchable fire".[153]

In contrast to all this, Jesus' message was one of good news, and the setting up of his kingdom was to be a time of great rejoicing. For Jesus, the kingdom meant "good tidings to the poor ... and recovering of sight to the blind, to set at liberty them that are bruised, to proclaim the acceptable year of the Lord".[154] Later some of the Apostles wrote about the kingdom in similar terms. Paul declared, "The kingdom of God is ... righteousness and peace and joy in the Holy Spirit";[155] and Peter wrote of "him who called you out of darkness into his marvelous light".[156]

Jesus also indicated that one of the important requirements for entrance into the kingdom is repentance.

He said, "Repent; for the kingdom of heaven is at hand".[157]

The word repent refers to a complete change in our thoughts, attitudes, and actions; and it was used by both John the Baptizer and Jesus. However, with John the Baptizer repentance was associated with the possibility of punishment for wrongdoing; the implied warning was, "Repent ... or else!" But with Jesus, while repentance called for a letting go of wrong beliefs and erroneous ways of living, it also included entering into the new and joyous experiences of the kingdom.

---

[153] Matthew 3:12
[154] Luke 4:18-19
[155] Romans 14:17
[156] I Peter 2:9
[157] Matthew 4:17

At this time the following statements regarding the kingdom should be given careful consideration:

"The kingdom of heaven, or of the heavens, is a state of consciousness in which the soul and body are in harmony with Divine Mind".[158]

"Jesus [said] ... 'The kingdom of God is within you.' This kingdom is now ready. 'The fields ... are white already unto harvest.' The conditions are ripe. But only those come in who are willing to exchange for it their ideas of earthly possessions".[159]

"When a person arrives at a certain exalted consciousness through the exercise of his mind in thinking about God and his laws, he is lifted above the thoughts of the world into a heavenly realm. This is the beginning of his entry into the kingdom of the heavens, which was the text of many of Jesus' discourses. When a man attains this high place in consciousness he is baptized by the Spirit; that is, his mind and even his body are suffused with spiritual essences, and he begins the process of becoming a new creature in Christ Jesus".[160]

Having considered the message of Jesus, we should now give attention to:

Jesus' Methods of Teaching.

In presenting his message of the kingdom, as discussed above, Jesus did not limit himself to the bare statement given in Mark 1:14-15. Jesus' kingdom message was presented in many different ways, and under many

---

[158] *Metaphysical Bible Dictionary*, p. 266
[159] Fillmore, Charles *Keep a True Lent*, p. 176
[160] Fillmore, Charles Teach Us to Pray, p. 163

different circumstances; and in making these presentations Jesus used several different teaching methods. At this time, therefore, it will be helpful to make a careful study of the teaching methods used by Jesus, selecting four outstanding examples. Such a study will lead us to a better understanding, not only of the kingdom message, but also of the entire ministry of Jesus.

Teaching by Precept
Read the passages: Matthew 11:28; Mark 2:27; Luke 8:19-21; John 8:31-32

The word precept has been defined as "a commandment, instruction, or order, intended as a rule of action or conduct ... a practical rule guiding behavior, technique, etc." However, for purposes of Christian Scripture study, we may regard the word precept as indicating a short statement of Truth, given without embellishment or illustration and intended to convey important instruction to the hearer or reader. Some of the precepts of Jesus take the form of invitations or promises.

Look again at the Sermon on the Mount[161] and note how many of these "precepts" or sayings of Jesus, as they are sometimes called, are to be found in these three chapters. The opening section of the Sermon, often referred to as the Beatitudes, begins with the words:

> *Blessed are the poor in spirit: for theirs is the kingdom of heaven.*[162]

---

[161] Matthew 5, 6, 7
[162] Matthew 5:3

Then notice how precept after precept occurs throughout the entire Sermon. The following are good examples:

"Judge not, that ye be not judged".[163]

"Ask, and it shall be given you; seek, and ye shall find; knock, and it shall be opened unto you".[164]

"All things therefore whatsoever ye would that men should do unto you, even so do ye also unto them: for this is the law and the prophets".[165]

Similar precepts are plentiful throughout the four Gospels, and we should become thoroughly familiar with this type of teaching, seeking to trace, wherever possible, the connection between these precepts and Jesus' message of the kingdom.

Teaching by Parables
Read the passages: Matthew 13:1-58; 25:14-30; Luke 10:25-37; 15:1-32

An outstanding teaching method employed by Jesus was his use of parables. These parables have a prominent place in the Synoptic Gospels, and Jesus used them freely throughout his ministry. Matthew states, "All these things spoke Jesus in parables unto the multitudes; and without a parable spoke he nothing unto them".[166]

It should be noted here that the parables of Jesus are found mainly in the Synoptic Gospels.[167] John's Gospel

---

[163] Matthew 7:1
[164] Matthew 7:7
[165] Matthew 7:12
[166] Matthew 13:34
[167] Matthew, Mark and Luke

contains two or three suggestions of parables, but these differ considerably from the parables recorded by the synoptic writers. John's Gospel deals with what is sometimes termed the advanced, or deeper, teachings of Jesus; and since the Synoptic Gospels were already in circulation, the writer may have felt it unnecessary to duplicate the parables. However, in our next lesson we shall see how the writer of John's Gospel used an altogether different type of material to take the place of parables.

Perhaps the best way of entering into an understanding of the parables will be by asking, and seeking to briefly answer, a few leading questions, as follows:

What is a Parable?

A parable is a short story dealing with familiar subjects or situations, and is told for the purpose of illustrating or making clear some important truth or phase of teaching. Thus, the value of the parable is to be found not in the actual story, but in the truth or teaching which it pictorially presents. A popular definition is: "A parable is an earthly story with a heavenly meaning."

Why did Jesus use Parables in His Teaching?

At first glance, this seems a very simple question, and the answer appears self-evident. Above, it was stated that the purpose of a parable is to illustrate or make clear some important teaching. Parables may be likened to pictures in a book, or illustrations in a sermon; their main purpose is to help people grasp the truth. Thus, when we ask, "Why did Jesus use parables?" the apparent answer is: Jesus used parables so that people could easily understand the important points in his teaching.

However, referring to Matthew 13, we find that the very question we are discussing here was originally put to Jesus by his own disciples. "The disciples came, and said unto him, why do you speak unto them in parables?" Jesus gave the following cryptic reply: "Unto you it is given to know the mysteries of the kingdom of heaven, but to them it is not given. ... Therefore, I speak to them in parables; because seeing they see not, and hearing they hear not, neither do they understand".[168]

How are we to interpret the above statement?

First, we must recognize that among the thronging crowds surrounding Jesus there were many persons who listened to him merely to pass the time, or for the purpose of being entertained. They had no real interest in the kingdom message of Jesus. Hence, all such persons would continue to hear, but they would not really understand. However, Jesus knew that among those self-same crowds there were some earnest souls who were really seeking the truth; and as these seekers listened to the parables, they would eventually be led into an understanding of the kingdom.

Second, it must also be recognized that some of Jesus' parables constituted what may be termed a kindly method of reproof. These parables were directed toward certain groups, or individuals, for the purpose of correcting their erroneous ways of thinking. Of course, the important

---

[168] Matthew 13:10, 11, 13

lessons in these parables would be helpful to all of Jesus' hearers; but the persons immediately concerned would recognize a special message for themselves. Thus, Matthew 21: 45 reads: "And when the chief priests and the Pharisees heard his parables, they perceived that he spoke of them." In other words (to use the terms of the old proverb) they saw that the shoe fitted, and they must needs wear it! Examples of this type of parable are "the Two Sons,"[169] "the Wicked Husbandmen",[170] and "the Prodigal Son".[171]

One other point should be considered: Just prior to the coming of Jesus, John the Baptizer had adopted a denunciatory style of preaching. John placed great emphasis on the sins of the people, and spoke to them in stern terms. Jesus, however, adopted an entirely different style in proclaiming his kingdom message. Instead of warning people of "the wrath to come," he tried to interest people and win them to his way of thinking. Thus it was that he taught in parables, presenting his message in terms that were acceptable and helpful. True, there came a time when Jesus himself used the denunciatory style of speaking—as when he called the Pharisees "hypocrites"[172] —but this was only after he had used the parable method.

---

[169] Matthew 21:28-32
[170] Matthew 21:33-41
[171] Luke 15:11-32
[172] Mark 7:6

What is the best way to study the parables?

Let us now outline a practical plan of study, in order that we may obtain a good grasp, not only of the parables themselves, but also of their meaning and purpose. At the end of the lesson will be found a list of Jesus' parables and some suggestions showing how the proposed plan of study may be put into operation. But first let us list the necessary steps in studying the parables:

1. Read carefully the parable to be studied. Do not omit this first step. Many of the parables are so familiar that we may assume that a re-reading is unnecessary. But this very familiarity may have its own disadvantages and dangers; so it will be well to read carefully each parable, no matter how familiar it may seem.

2. Try to get a clear picture of the setting of the parable. This is very important. We should ask: Under what circumstances did Jesus utter this parable? What was actually happening at that time? Was Jesus directing this parable to any particular person or group? If so, what was his purpose in so doing? In other words, we should gather as much information as possible concerning each parable. Usually, the answers to the suggested questions are indicated in the context, so the setting can easily be reconstructed. But even in the few instances where the circumstances are not too clear, a careful reading will disclose enough

information to form some sort of helpful background.

3. Try to pick out the theme, or main teaching, of the parable. This will not be difficult if we have the right setting or background. We should ask: What is the real message contained in this parable? What particular point, or special teaching, was Jesus seeking to put forward at this time? What important truth does this parable illustrate? Usually the answers to these or similar questions give us the theme of the parable. However, one point should be noted: As a general rule, each parable contains only one main idea; but, since the parable is in story form, there will also be included a number of details, making for color and interest in the story. Hence we must learn to focus our attention on the theme, or main teaching, and not be led away into any bypaths suggested by details. This is most important if we would really profit from a study of the parables.

4. Additional interest is found in seeking to trace the connection between the parables and Jesus' teaching of the kingdom. It will be well to ask: What special point in the kingdom teaching is illustrated by this parable? How does this parable help us better to understand and find entrance into the kingdom? In many instances a definite connection can be traced; and the time and effort thus put forth will return rich

dividends in a deeper understanding, both of
the parables and of the kingdom.

5. As a final step in the study of the parables, we
    should seek to understand their metaphysical
    meaning. This is important, because we are
    thus led to see the great value of the parables
    and profit from their teachings. The steps
    already suggested enable us to see what the
    parables meant in the days of Jesus' ministry;
    but this final, or metaphysical, step brings their
    message right home to us in terms of practical,
    present-day living.

The following suggestions should prove helpful in
finding the metaphysical interpretation of the parables:

Try to get a clear understanding of the theme, or
main teaching, of the parable. This understanding is
important, since the entire interpretation of the parable
arises out of the theme.

Recognize that the parable pictorially represents
some phase in the development of our consciousness. As a
story, the parable seems to be dealing with happenings
taking place in the outside world; but in a metaphysical
sense, these happenings are regarded as taking place
within our own consciousness.

Realize that all persons, places, or activities in the
parable are symbols of ideas, qualities, or powers active
within us. Thus, we are not to regard one person in the
parable as representing self, while another person
represents someone else. All persons, places, and activities
have their location as symbols within self. For example,

the prodigal son and his elder brother represent ideas and activities in our life and affairs; under certain conditions, both may be functioning in our consciousness.[173]

Remember to relate all details in the parable to the central theme, as suggested above. The theme contains the really important teaching, and the details should be used only to explain, amplify, or otherwise help us to understand and apply the theme. We should continue to ask self: What special idea, or message, was Jesus here seeking to present? How does this apply to us today? This procedure will give meaning and purpose to each parable, as applied to our own life and affairs; and it will also guard against fanciful or far-fetched interpretation of details.

Refer to the list of Jesus' parables, as given in appendix A. Read these carefully and select several for further study.

Refer also to appendix B, which gives several examples showing how the directions for study given above may be applied to specific parables. The principles given may be similarly applied to all parables, to bring out their important lessons for us today.

---

[173] See examples given in appendix B for further explanation.)

Chapter 7 - The Teaching Ministry of Jesus (Part Two)

Historical Questions

1. Explain briefly the purpose of Jesus' miracles. Why are these miracles given such a prominent place in the Gospels?

2. How would you define a miracle? Mention some differences between earlier ideas of miracles and our present understanding.

3. Explain briefly how in John's Gospel miracles are used to illustrate some important teachings of Jesus. Give instances, with Scripture references.

4. In your own words tell the story of Jesus changing the water into wine. (John 2:1-11) Do not attempt to interpret the miracle, but simply tell what happened at Cana.

5. Which miracle is recorded in all four Gospels? Can you suggest any reason for this fourfold recording?

Metaphysical Questions

1. Several important teachings are presented and emphasized in Jesus' miracles of healing. Mention and briefly explain three of these teachings, giving Scripture references in each instance.

2. The Gospels record several miracles of Jesus healing blindness. What does blindness symbolize in our experience? When and how does healing take place?

3. List and briefly explain several important steps for demonstrating supply as indicated in Jesus' miracle of feeding the five thousand.

4. Using your own words, tell briefly the story of Jesus stilling the storm. (Mark 4:35-41) What does this miracle represent in our experience?

5. How would you explain the story of Jesus withering the fig tree? (See Matt. 21:18-22.) What is the important lesson in this miracle? How does this apply to us?

Lesson Text

In chapter six we saw how Jesus presented his message of the kingdom through precepts and parables. But it was also indicated that four methods of presentation would be discussed. This lesson deals with the two remaining methods used by Jesus. Already we have before us the general heading: "Jesus' Methods of Teaching," with the two subdivisions as mentioned above: "Teaching by Precepts," and "Teaching by Parables." Now we come to the third subdivision:

Teaching through Miracles

Read the passages: John 8:12-18; John 9:1-41

The Gospels record some thirty-five miracles performed by Jesus, and many of these are quite well known. In all probability, Jesus performed other miracles which are not recorded, and there is a hint of this toward the close of John's Gospel;[174] but there are enough

---

[174] See John 20:30

recorded in the Gospels to give us a good working basis for a thorough study of the miracles.

Sometimes people ask: "Why did Jesus perform miracles? Why are the miracles given such a prominent place in the Gospels?" The answer usually given is that the purpose of the miracles was to prove, or bear witness to, the divinity of Jesus. Jesus must have been divine, so it was argued, otherwise he could not have accomplished such marvelous works! In point of fact, Jesus himself suggested something of this sort, when he said, "Believe me for the very works' sake".[175] There are also indications that some of the miracles were regarded as practical expressions of Jesus' great compassion. We read: "he had compassion on them, and healed their sick".[176]

However, we should recognize a further purpose in Jesus' miracles. There are many indications in the Gospels that Jesus performed miracles to explain and emphasize his teaching. Sometimes the precepts and parables were not fully understood. Even Jesus' disciples at times failed to comprehend his deeper teachings. Jesus saw that the truth he was seeking to impart must be taught in some other way. Thus, many of Jesus' miracles may be regarded as truth-teaching presented in practical form. In other words, the miracles were what we sometimes term "object lessons"; and their purpose was to make some of the deeper teachings of Jesus self-evident to all persons concerned.

The writer of John's Gospel clearly saw this connection between the teachings and the miracles of

---

[175] John 14:11
[176] Matthew 14:14

Jesus. Thus, in the first Scripture passage given at the beginning of this section we read that Jesus declared, "I am the light of the world".[177] To us, of course, this is a familiar piece of teaching; but to Jesus' hearers it must have sounded strange and difficult to understand. We find this statement closely followed by the account of Jesus' miracle of healing the man born blind.[178] Surely, no better illustration or explanation of the teaching could be given! In the miracle Jesus was pointing out that his statement about being "the light of the world" was not a mere figure of speech; for truly he was indeed the light-bringer to all those who sit in darkness and in the shadow of death.

That the above-mentioned connection is not a mere coincidence is shown by the fact that several similar pairings are given in John's Gospel. For example: Jesus' teaching, "I am the bread of life",[179] is closely associated with the miracle of feeding the five thousand;[180] Jesus' statement, "I am the resurrection, and the life",[181] is immediately followed by the miracle of raising Lazarus from the tomb.[182] There are also a number of other instances where Jesus clearly used his miracles to illustrate or provide what may be termed practical examples for his teaching.

At this point we may find ourselves inquiring: "What is a miracle? How should we think of the miracles

---

[177] John 8:12
[178] John 9:1-41
[179] John 6:35
[180] John 6:1-14
[181] John 11:25
[182] John 11:38-44

recorded in the Gospels?" A helpful definition may, therefore, be in order.

In times past, miracles were regarded as happenings brought about by some super-natural agency and having no connection with the laws of cause and effect. But nowadays most persons are coming to recognize that "miracles are events that take place as the result of the application of a higher law to certain conditions".[183] However, if we are to understand and profit by the miracles recorded in the Gospels, something should be added to the above definition. We should recognize not only the underlying cause of miracles but also their purpose. Jesus' miracles may be defined as extraordinary happenings brought about by the operation of higher laws, performed both to help those persons immediately concerned and to present, emphasize, or make clear certain important teachings helpful to all persons.

We are now in a position to undertake a careful study of the miracles themselves.

At the outset it will be noted that Jesus' miracles fall into four main groups:

1. Miracles of healing
2. Miracles of supply
3. Miracles overcoming death
4. Nature miracles.

Let us consider the miracles in this order:

---

[183] Fillmore, Charles *Keep a True Lent*, p. 178

First: Jesus' Miracles of Healing.

Read the passage: Section 1, "Healing Miracles of Jesus" in the appendix.

Jesus' miracles of healing form by far the largest of the four groups mentioned above, with some twenty-three healings recorded in the Gospels. For purposes of study, these healing miracles have been divided into four sections;[184] and a good study plan would be as follows:

1. Read carefully the miracles listed in Section One as suggested above. It will be noticed that all these miracles are recorded in Matthew's Gospel. However, take a few extra minutes to check the corresponding accounts as given in the other Gospels.[185] Do not be in a hurry when reading these miracle stories. In some instances, details of the miracles will vary in the different Gospels; and these variations should be noted.

2. Follow the same procedure with Sections Two, Three, and Four. Some of the miracles are recorded in only one Gospel; but where there are duplicate accounts, the differences should be carefully considered. However, in each case, try to get a good grasp of the story as a whole.

3. When reading these accounts of the miracles we should always keep in mind what was mentioned earlier, regarding the purpose of the

---

[184] See Appendix C
[185] For Scripture references see Appendix.

miracles. This is very important. Jesus' miracles were performed, not only to help the persons immediately concerned, but also to present and emphasize some very important lessons. It is to be hoped that these lessons were recognized by the persons helped; but the miracles of Jesus go far beyond this, and provide lessons for all persons and for all times. Some of these important lessons may now be indicated:

The healing miracles present and emphasize the teaching that God's kingdom is a kingdom of wholeness and peace, and that health is the inheritance of all God's children. During his ministry Jesus said, "I am come ... not to do mine own will, but the will of him that sent me".[186] All Jesus' healing work must, therefore, be recognized as an out-picturing of God. Through his healing miracles Jesus was saying, in effect, "God's will is not sickness or inharmony of any sort, but health and wholeness." Jesus said, further, "It is not the will of your Father ... that one of these little ones should perish".[187]

The healing miracles also place great emphasis upon faith. Faith is the great essential, if there is to be a healing. Many statements to this effect are to be found in the accounts of the healing miracles "Do you believe that I am able to do this?"[188] "Your faith hath made you whole"[189] "All things are possible to him that believes";[190]

---

[186] John 6:38
[187] Matthew 18:14
[188] Matthew 9:28
[189] Luke 8:48
[190] Mark 9:23

"I have not found so great faith, no, not in Israel".[191] On the other hand, the Gospels clearly indicate that lack of faith holds off healing. Indeed, we are told that "he [Jesus] did not many mighty works there, because of their unbelief".[192]

In some accounts of healing miracles there are suggestions regarding the cause of physical inharmony, and emphasis is placed on the necessity for forgiveness. To the man sick of the palsy, Jesus said, "Son, thy sins are forgiven";[193] and to the helpless man at the pool, Jesus said, "Sin no more, lest a worse thing befall thee".[194]

We usually think of the healing miracles as being instantaneous, with the sufferer making immediate recovery. However, there are some exceptions to this general rule; and in such cases the healing came by degrees.[195] These exceptions should be carefully studied for causes of this seeming delay. Possibly there is a twofold lesson here:

1. Healing may be proportionate to our capacity to receive; and
2. We must persevere, even in such matters as healing.

Some healing miracles emphasize the importance of thanksgiving in connection with healing. The story of the ten lepers is the classic example of giving thanks, and also of forgetting to give thanks.[196] This lesson of

---

[191] Matthew 8:10
[192] Matthew 13:58
[193] Mark 2:5
[194] John 5:14
[195] See Mark 8:22-26; John 9:1-7
[196] Luke 17:11-19

thanksgiving may also be recognized in several other healing miracles, if we take time to "read between the lines." By a similar process we may see the work of denial and affirmation in these miracles.

Metaphysical Interpretation of Miracles

Carefully reread the notes given in chapter six regarding metaphysical interpretation of the parables. Most of the principles there given also apply to the interpretation of miracles. However, when studying the miracles it will be well to recognize several additional features, which may be summarized as follows:

The need: In healing miracles it is easy to see that the need is for healing of some sort. There is something missing, and the supply of that "something" constitutes the miracle. Of course, the nature of the supply varies according to circumstances; but with the supply forthcoming, the result is wholeness or health.

In the healing miracles, as recorded in the Gospels, the need is mostly of physical character, and the references are easy to understand. We must, however, recognize these physical ailments as symbols of mental or spiritual conditions prevailing in our consciousness. For example: Several miracles deal with physical blindness. But in our experience we are often called upon to deal with a different sort of blindness. Jesus, speaking to his disciples, once asked, "Having eyes, do you see not?"[197] And are there not many important things in life which we fail to see, even though we have good physical sight? Sometimes we fail to see splendid opportunities or other good

_____

[197] Mark 8:18

awaiting us, and we do not recognize our spiritual possibilities. Whenever we find ourselves exclaiming, "I can't see this!" or "I can't see that!" we are like the blind men mentioned in the miracles. Other physical infirmities may also be recognized as symbols of mental or spiritual conditions where there is "something missing." Not only are there sick bodies, but there are sick souls which cry out for healing!

The healer: When reading the Gospel stories of the healings, our first impression is that two or more persons are involved. First, there is the person in need of healing, and then there is Jesus, the Healer. Historically, this is a correct summary of the situation; and reading of this sort is always interesting and inspiring. However, we should now realize that just as the person in need resides within our consciousness, so does the healing power also abide within us. Certainly, Scripture tells of the healing work of Jesus in the long ago; but Scripture also points clearly to "Christ in you, the hope of glory".[198] In a physical way we may find ourselves thinking in terms of outer activities; from the metaphysical viewpoint, we must now recognize that our true healer is the indwelling Christ. Charles Fillmore states: "Christ is declaring, 'I am the light of the world.' When our blind, stumbling thoughts awaken to the reality of the Christ, darkness falls away and we see clearly".[199]

---

[198] Colossians 1:27
[199] Fillmore, Charles *Mysteries of John*, p. 96

Second: Jesus' Miracles of Supply

Read the passages: John 6:1-15. (Compare with: Matthew 14: 13-23; Mark 6:30-46; Luke 9:10-17.)

Having considered Jesus' miracles of healing, we now turn our attention to his miracles of supply. Six miracles of this type are recorded in the Gospels. Scripture references for one of these miracles of supply are given above; and references for the other five can be found at the end of this lesson.

Jesus' miracle of feeding the five thousand makes a good start for a brief study of the miracles of supply. The Gospel writer, in giving the account of this miracle, first calls attention to the seriousness of the situation. Something was urgently needed; and the supply of that "something" constituted the miracle. A similar pattern is followed in the accounts of the other miracles of supply.

Bearing in mind what was suggested earlier regarding the purpose of the miracles, we shall find in the story of feeding the five thousand some very important, practical, present-day lessons. Jesus shows us here how to meet emergencies, and how to demonstrate abundant supply, even in the face of seeming lack. Thus this miracle may be termed "a pattern for supply." Note the following clearly defined steps:

1. Preparation: The Gospels indicate how Jesus, long before this miracle, had built into his consciousness the thought of God as omnipresent supply. In connection with his first temptation Jesus emphasized the idea of feeding from "every word that proceeds out of

the mouth of God".[200] Then, speaking to his disciples, Jesus said, "I have meat [food] to eat that ye know not".[201] Furthermore, Jesus so identified himself with this omnipresent supply, that he was able to say, "I am the bread of life".[202]

2. Demonstrating supply: At this point the story of the miracle should be reread John 6:1-15, and a careful check made of the on-the-spot steps taken by Jesus. Note the following: Jesus recognized what may be termed a "nucleus" of supply in the five barley loaves and two fishes. With us, when facing lack, there is a tendency to say that nothing is available; but this miracle indicates that there is always something—even though that "something" may be small! Jesus established order and aroused expectancy when he bade the people sit down. Note further how Jesus gave thanks, even before the actual appearance of supply. Jesus also encouraged his disciples to exercise their faith by attempting what appeared to be an impossibility. Note, finally, that this was no mere "token meal," but that all present were abundantly supplied. Can we not take similar steps when supply is needed?

3. An important afterthought: Many persons wonder why Jesus instructed his disciples to

---

[200] Matthew 4:4
[201] John 4:32
[202] John 6:35

"gather up the broken fragments." Evidently this was more than a matter of "tidying up"; and certainly there was no thought of saving these "leftovers" for later use. It would seem that Jesus was here placing emphasis upon what had taken place. He knew that it was easy for people to forget, and he took this step in order that the miracle would be well-remembered by the disciples. In modern times this type of action is often referred to as a process of "impressing the subconscious." The effectiveness of this action is indicated by the fact that this is the only miracle recorded in all four Gospels. Other miracles were referred to in the Early Church; but this miracle must have been discussed so often that all four Gospel writers felt that it was "required reading," and must be included in their records!

The remaining miracles of supply should now be read, and all important points carefully noted.[203] It should be recognized that in these miracles there is the oft-repeated teaching that God's kingdom is a kingdom of abundance; and when we call upon him in faith, our needs are met in a manner "exceeding abundantly above all that we ask or think, according to the power that works in us".[204]

---

[203] Scripture references are given in the appendix.
[204] Ephesians 3:20

Third: Jesus' Miracles Overcoming Death

Read the passages: John 10:7-18; John 11:1-46; Matthew 9:18-26; Mark 5:21-43; Luke 8:40-56; Luke 7:11-17

Before attempting to study the miracles wherein Jesus overcame death, it will be well to read John 10:7-18, as suggested above. Note especially verses 10, 17, and 18. In the first instance, Jesus clearly states his purpose: "I came that they may have life ... abundantly"; while the second statement indicates that Jesus is preparing to implement these miracles with a personal demonstration.

The basic idea in these three miracles is that of life. God's kingdom is a kingdom of life, and the experience that we refer to as death has no place therein. It should be noted how Jesus carefully avoids the use of the word death, and how he recognizes that this is only a temporary condition, to be followed by an awakening into life. We may regard all this as an amplification of an earlier statement by the Gospel writer: "In him was life; and the life was the light of men".[205]

Metaphysically, these miracles of overcoming death are very important. In our experience, there are times when something seems to die within us. Our youthful energies, hopes, ambitions, or imaginations lose their freshness and vigor and tend to become dormant or "lifeless." In this connection, it should be noted that two of the miracles in this group deal with young people. However, maturity also has similar problems; and this is made clear in the miracle of raising Lazarus. The name Lazarus means "One whom God helps" or "help of God."

---

[205] John 1:4

But this reliance upon God's help and guidance, and all similar spiritual ideas and activities may become dormant or "die" within us. However, even in such a situation, the indwelling Christ is able to speak the restoring word, so that our "Lazarus" does indeed "come forth." The Apostle Paul was referring to something similar to this, when he exclaimed: "Awake, thou that sleep, and arise from the dead, and Christ shall shine upon thee".[206]

The miracle of raising Jairus' daughter[207] and other references should be carefully studied, since it contains helpful information for all who would continue this restoring work. We should recall that Jesus instructed us not only to "heal the sick" but also to "raise the dead".[208] When we also recognize that all such work must begin within our own consciousness, the words and actions of Jesus, as recorded in connection with this miracle, will take on new significance. Note the following:

1. What Jesus did: Jesus took with him Peter, John, and James. This indicates that faith, love, and wisdom (or discriminating judgment) have an important part in the work of restoration, Jesus also shut the door of the house, ostensibly to keep out the unbelieving neighbors and professional mourners. We also need to shut the door of our consciousness to keep out all negative thoughts and such discouraging words as "It can't be done!"

---

[206] Ephesians 5:14
[207] Matthew 9:18-26
[208] Matthew 10:8

2. What Jesus said: Speaking to Jairus, Jesus said, "Fear not, and only believe." We too must learn to replace fear with faith, even when the situation seems hopeless, Jesus said further, "She is not dead, but sleeps." Here is use of denial and affirmation, overcoming the seeming and establishing the real.

3. Two later actions by Jesus: The account tells how Jesus took the little girl by the hand and said to her, "Damsel, I say unto thee, Arise." This action shows that Jesus expected something to happen as the result of his statement. he did not sit back and await possible developments, but acted in accord with his spoken word, note the further suggestion that something to eat be given to the girl. Physically and spiritually it is not enough just to arouse the slumbering spirit; some further action must be taken to insure increasing strength and continuing activity.

Fourth: Jesus' Nature Miracles

Read the passages: Matthew 8:23-27; Mark 4:35-41; Luke 8:22-25; Matthew 14:24-36; Mark 6:47-56; John 6:16-21; Matthew 21:18-22; Mark 11:20-25

The miracles which compose this small group are usually referred to as "nature miracles," for two reasons:

1. The other miracles of Jesus deal with human beings or situations involving human beings; but these miracles deal with things

belonging to the realm of nature;—the Lake of Galilee, a growing tree.

2. The higher laws invoked in these miracles appear to cut through or transcend the laws that govern the activities of the natural elements.

Fortunately, the important lessons contained in these nature miracles are not difficult to grasp. When we read of Jesus stilling the storm, we realize that storms also arise within our own consciousness and in our relationships, causing us to become anxious and fearful. However, the indwelling Christ ever journeys with us, and when we call upon him, he calms the storm with his "Peace, be still!" We recognize that the story of Jesus walking on the water is really a lesson concerning faith. Note especially the near failure of Peter (faith), and how the outstretched hand of Jesus saved him from sinking. Perhaps it was an experience of this sort which caused the hymn writer to exclaim: "Hold Thou my hand; for then, O loving Savior, No dread of ill shall make my soul afraid."

The miracle of withering the fig tree is just a little more complicated, and the reader may find himself asking: "Why did Jesus do this?" Actually, at first reading the miracle does appear somewhat in the nature of a petulant action brought about by reason of disappointment and frustration. However, we do not associate this sort of thing with the ministry of Jesus! What, then, shall we think of this miracle?

As a first step, we should refer back to the parable of the barren fig tree, as given in Luke 13:6-9. In this instance the lesson is quite clear. The fig tree in this parable represents the nation of Israel, and the barren condition of the tree indicates Israel's failure to accomplish its God-ordained purpose.   However, it would appear that the teaching given in this parable had not sunk very deeply into the minds of the disciples. Hence, Jesus now repeated the parable in objective form and in such a dramatic way that it could not fail to register with the disciples. A story about a tree could be heard and forgotten; but a tree stricken down in this startling way could never be forgotten! In other words, the miracle of withering the fig tree is to be regarded as an emphatic restatement of the important lesson given earlier in the parable. Historically, the fulfillment of this prediction regarding the unfruitful tree is seen in the complete overthrow of Jerusalem a few years later, 70 CE.

The lesson for us in all this is quite clear: We readily recognize that the purpose of the fig tree is to bear fruit, and unless this purpose is accomplished the tree is useless and is cut down. Similarly, the follower of Jesus Christ is expected to "bear fruit"— that is, to show forth the Christ Spirit in his life and activities. Jesus said, "Herein is my Father glorified, that ye bear much fruit; and so shall ye be my disciples".[209] Without such "fruit," life loses its purpose. A similar teaching appears in the well-known parable of the talents.[210]

Teaching through Actions
Read the passage: John 13:1-20

---

[209] John 15:8
[210] Matthew 25:14-30

Thus far, in considering Jesus' teaching methods, we have seen that he taught through precepts, parables, and miracles. A fourth teaching method should now be recognized. We should recognize that Jesus taught through his day-by-day activities, and that his teaching was not by words only, but also by his deeds. Unless we are on the lookout for this action type of teaching, we may miss some very important lessons in Jesus' ministry. Note how, in the suggested reading given above, Jesus himself called attention to this type of teaching, when he said: "Do you know what I have done to you? ... I have given you an example".[211]

Perhaps at this point we should make clear what is indicated by the term "Teaching through Actions." Certain actions are recorded in connection with some of the miracles—such as putting clay on the eyes of the blind man, breaking the bread when feeding the five thousand, and so on. Such actions form part of the miracle, and they should be so considered. But, during his ministry, Jesus performed a number of actions which, when rightly understood, have within them some very important teaching. Indeed, careful reading of the Gospels indicates that Jesus' main purpose in performing these actions was to present the teaching in such a way that actions spoke louder than words! Several instances of this action-teaching have already been given in these lessons—but it will be well to reread the following:

1. Jesus' Baptism in Matthew 3:13-17
2. The Temptations in Matthew 4:1-11
3. Cleansing the Temple in John 2:13-22

---

[211] John 13:12-15

4. Leaving Judea and going to Galilee in John 4:1-4

It would be well also to note Jesus' actions in dealing with some of the "lost sheep," as recorded in the Gospels, and try to understand the lessons contained in such actions. The following are good instances:

1. Jesus' association with publicans and sinners in Matthew 9:10-13
2. The woman taken in adultery in John 8:1-11
3. The Samaritan woman in John 4:5-26

Other important instances of Jesus' teaching through his actions will be given in subsequent chapters.

Chapter 8 - The Gathering Storm

Historical Questions

1. Explain briefly what brought about the rejection of Jesus. In your answer give (a) the traditional explanation, and (b) what appears to be the real reason for the rejection.

2. Did Jesus say that he was planning to destroy the Temple buildings? (See John 2:19.) Briefly explain the situation, and bring out the real meaning of Jesus' statement.

3. Why were the people disturbed when Jesus spoke about the laws of Moses? (Matt. 5) Explain briefly how Jesus put new meaning into these laws.

4. Why did the Pharisees complain about the actions of Jesus' disciples? (Mark 2:23-28) What important statement regarding the Sabbath did Jesus give on that occasion?

5. What important decision was made by the Jewish leaders immediately following the raising of Lazarus? (John 11:47-57) What reasons did they give for their proposed course of action?

Metaphysical Questions

1. At the trial of Jesus, Pontius Pilate asked an important question. (Matt. 27:22) What does this question mean to us today?

2. What does the cleansing of the Temple symbolize in the development of our consciousness? How is the cleansing of our temple accomplished?

3. Jesus, speaking of his body temple, said: "I will raise it up." (John 2:19) How do we raise our consciousness?

4. Give a brief explanation of Jesus' statement, "I came not to destroy, but to fulfill." (Matt. 5:17)

5. How may we enter into the rest and peace of the true Sabbath?

Lesson Text

This lesson is divided into three main sections, and these should be studied in the order given. At the outset it will be noted that these sections are not arranged in chronological sequence; the first section deals with the final rejection of Jesus, while the second and third sections deal with activities that led up to the rejection. In other words, we first take a good look at the "storm"—to use the language of the lesson title—and then we plunge into the underlying currents that were responsible for stirring up the storm. However, you will discover that this procedure greatly helps when studying this section of the Christian Scriptures, and leads to a better grasp of all the factors involved in the rejection of Jesus. Furthermore, a careful study of this "gathering storm" in the way suggested will make the best possible preparation for the important lesson that is to follow.

Read the passages: Matthew 16:21-28; Matthew 21:33-46; Luke 13:22-35

The Rejection of Jesus

In this study of the Christian Scriptures we have now reached the point where we are called upon to face the fact of the rejection of Jesus. Thus far we have seen how Jesus was engaged in presenting his kingdom teaching, performing miracles, and doing other good works; and for a while his activities were greeted with public acclaim. Indeed, people were asking, "Is not this the Messiah?" But then came a complete change. Popularity gave place to a gathering storm of opposition. Jesus' teachings, claims, and good works proved totally unacceptable. The Jewish leaders denounced him as an impostor; while the common people, who aforetime had "heard him gladly," now joined in the ever-increasing clamor for his destruction. The gospel writer aptly sums up the situation by stating, "He came unto his own, and they that were his own received him not".[212]

The question arises: Why was Jesus thus rejected? From our present-day viewpoint it would seem that Jesus fully demonstrated his divine Sonship, and that his messianic claims were well-founded. Even the centurion who officiated at the Crucifixion is reported as saying, "Truly this man was the Son of God".[213] Why, then, was this divinity not generally recognized? Why was Jesus rejected?

This question calls for careful consideration.

First, it will be well to recall the traditional teaching that Jesus was rejected because he did not measure up to the messianic expectations of the people. Great things were expected of the coming Messiah; but as Jesus' ministry developed, people saw that their hopes were not being fulfilled. Jesus did not proclaim himself to be the

---

[212] John 1:11
[213] Mark 15:39

warrior-leader who would overthrow the Romans and set up the new kingdom of Israel. Nor did he claim to be the supernatural "Messenger," coming down from the heavens and bringing all the kingdoms of the world under his dominion. Jesus did not concern himself with armed might and conquest; on the contrary, his teachings and actions were centered in love, peace, and good will. The people, therefore, were disappointed. Jesus did not measure up to the popular expectations, so he was rejected. This is the traditional explanation.

However, a careful reading of the Gospels leads to the realization that something needs to be added to what has been stated above. The Gospels indicate that the rejection of Jesus came about, not because he was something less than the Messiah the people expected, but because he proved himself to be much more of a Messiah than the people actually wanted! People expected the Messiah to inaugurate a new kingdom; but Jesus declared: "The kingdom of God is [in the midst of you]."[214] People expected the Messiah to change conditions in the land; but Jesus insisted that there must first be a change in the hearts of the people. The Messiah was expected to take up the sword against Rome; but Jesus said: "If any man would come after me, let him ... take up his cross, and follow me".[215] Many other similar instances will come to mind, showing how Jesus went far beyond anything expected. But the people would not accept Jesus' teaching and leadership, and they cried: "Away with him!" Thus it would seem that Jesus was rejected, not so much because he

---

[214] Luke 17:21
[215] Matthew 16:24

failed to measure up to expectations, but because his program was greater and more far-reaching than anything the people of his day were willing to accept.

From a present-day viewpoint, the rejection of Jesus has some very important implications. During Jesus' trial, Pontius Pilate asked, "What then shall I do unto Jesus who is called Christ?".[216] And this same question arises again in our experience today. In his teaching, Jesus presented what we now term the Christ way of life; and we can either reject or accept this teaching. If we are inclined toward rejection, we may seek to justify our action by claiming that the teaching is incorrect, fanciful, impractical, or even that it does not go far enough—just as the people did in the long ago. May it not be that the real reason for rejection lies in our inability, or unwillingness, to comprehend the nature and possibilities of Jesus' teaching? The teaching is good; but we may be unable, or unwilling, to see the good. However, there is always the better way—the way of acceptance—and the full acceptance of Jesus' teaching leads to a complete transformation of our life and affairs. James Russell Lowell emphasized the necessity for right decision in his challenging lines:

> "Once to every man and nation comes the moment to decide in the strife of Truth with Falsehood, for the good or evil side; Some great cause, God's new Messiah, offering each the bloom or blight and the choice goes by forever 'twixt that darkness and that light."

---

[216] Matthew 27:22

Read the passage: Mark 7:1-23; Luke 7:36-50; John 8:12-59; John 10:1-42

The Charges Brought against Jesus

Having considered the fact of Jesus' rejection, we should now give attention to the means used by his opponents to bring about this rejection. Of course, there was no open admission of the real reason for the rejection, such as was suggested above. Such an admission would be out of the question! Instead, a number of charges were formulated against Jesus, with the purpose of discrediting his teaching, and bringing his ministry to an end.

Apparently, the thought was that if the teaching could be discredited, then it would be a comparatively easy matter to dispose of the Teacher. The scripture passages given above indicate how rapidly the opposition toward Jesus was developing.

However, in addition to many general charges of false teaching, blasphemy, and so forth, something of a more serious nature began to take shape. Jesus' opponents charged that he was seeking to destroy the sacred institutions of Judaism, and that his teachings constituted a constant threat to the well-being of the whole nation. Hence, it was argued, if total disaster was to be averted, means must be found to speedily dispose of Jesus. Three specific institutions were mentioned as being in danger:

Jesus was charged with seeking to destroy the temple
Read the passage: John 2:13-23 (then compare with the following); Matt. 21:12-17; Mark 11:15-18; Luke 19:45-48

Jesus' activity in cleansing the Temple was discussed in chapter four, and at this time it will be well to reread the comments given there. However, we should now give special attention to some of Jesus' statements, as recorded in John's Gospel. Here, the gospel writer distinctly states that, "He [Jesus] spoke of the temple of his body"; and the indications are that Jesus must have spoken at some length, in order to make this point clear to all persons present. The gospel account shows that John fully understood the meaning of Jesus' words, so there seems no reason for any misunderstanding on the part of other persons present. Nevertheless, Jesus' opponents immediately seized upon the word destroy, and placed upon it their own false interpretation. Quickly then they spread the message: "This man Jesus is seeking to destroy our beloved Temple!" How far this false charge spread, and how deep was the impression made upon the minds of the people, is clearly shown by two subsequent events:

During the trial of Jesus, certain witnesses came forward, stating, "We heard him say, I will destroy this temple"[217] and when Jesus was crucified, people standing nearby cried out: "Thou that destroy the temple ... save thyself!"[218]

---

[217] Mark 14:58
[218] Matthew 27:40

At this point, the scripture passages given above should be carefully checked. It will be noticed that Mark and Luke indicate that the word destroy originated not with Jesus, but in the thoughts and activities of his opponents. We read: "And the chief priests and the scribes ... sought how they might destroy him [Jesus]".[219] Luke also uses the word destroy in a similar manner. May it not be, therefore, that John, in his account, was seeking to show how Jesus had picked up the thoughts and words of his opponents, and was plainly telling them that all their destructive efforts would be in vain? Jesus was saying, in effect: "You may seek to destroy my work, or even seek to destroy me; but what you thus destroy, I will surely raise up again! Just as this Temple has been rebuilt by Herod, so I will rebuild my body temple. Herod was forty-six years building this structure; but I will rebuild my temple in three days!" In this discussion Jesus was actually giving a restatement of an important message he had given on a previous occasion: "No one taketh it [my life] away from me. ... I have power to lay it down, and I have power to take it again".[220]

If we now place the various happenings in the order suggested above, the entire situation becomes clear:

1. Jesus "cleansed" the Temple—driving from the Temple courts the traders and money-changers doing business there.
2. The priests and the traders resented Jesus' action, since it took from them a large (but unlawful) income; and they then vowed to destroy him.

---

[219] Mark 11:18
[220] John 10:18

3. Jesus responded to this threat against his life by saying, "Destroy this temple, and in three days I will raise it up."

4. Jesus' opponents deliberately misinterpreted the word destroy, as used by Jesus, and circulated among the people the false charge that Jesus was seeking to destroy the Temple. This charge was calculated to arouse further opposition against Jesus, and bring his ministry to an end.

Two important metaphysical lessons arise out of these Temple activities:

Cleansing the Temple:

This should be recognized as a symbol of cleansing our consciousness. Just as Jesus swept the traders and money-changers from the Temple courts, so must we sweep from our consciousness all thoughts and conditions that are not in harmony with the divine plan. Much of this cleansing work can be accomplished through the use of denials; and we should make a careful study of this subject.[221]

"I will raise it up"[222]

In addition to the cleansing work mentioned above, there is also necessity for constructive activity. Mortal consciousness may seek to destroy our temple, but the work of the indwelling Christ is to raise it up. Hence there must be activity in raising, restoring, and rebuilding within

---

[221] Refer to *Lessons in Truth*, chapter on "Denials"; also, *Keep a True Lent*, chapter nine, "The Philosophy of Denial."
[222] John 2:19

our consciousness, until our body temple manifests perfection.[223] Much of this rebuilding work can be accomplished through the use of affirmative prayer. Therefore, in addition to the study of denials, as mentioned above, we should become familiar with the purpose and possibilities of affirmations.[224]

Jesus was charged with seeking to overthrow the system of laws and religious observances which had been given by Moses
Read the passages: John 6:22-71; John 7:1-52; Matthew 19:1-30; Matthew 22:23-46; Matthew 5:21-48; John 8:1-11

The second charge made against Jesus had reference to his day-by-day teaching. The Jewish leaders declared that Jesus, through his teaching, was seeking to overthrow the divinely ordained system of laws and religious observances which had been given to the people by Moses. This charge was brought against Jesus in many ways, and on many occasions; and the purpose of the charge was to discredit Jesus' teachings, and bring his ministry to an end. Again and again the cry was raised, "This Jesus is seeking to destroy the laws of Moses!" How effective and far-reaching this charge was is shown by the fact that it continued to circulate, even in the days of the early Church. The Book of Acts relates that at the trial of Stephen, the first martyr, certain witnesses declared: "We have heard him say, that this Jesus of Nazareth shall

---

[223] See Matthew 5:48
[224] See *Lessons in Truth*, lesson on "Affirmations"; also *Keep a True Lent*, chapter ten, "The Affirmative Word."

destroy this place, and shall change the customs which Moses delivered unto us".[225]

The scripture passages given above indicate how Jesus was called upon to carry on much of his ministry in an atmosphere of bitter controversy and violent personal attacks. True, there were times when "the common people heard him gladly";[226] but there were many other times when those same people violently disagreed with Jesus' teachings, and sought to bring his ministry to a sudden and tragic end. Much of this opposition can be traced to the charge that Jesus was seeking to change or destroy the laws given to the people by Moses.

We can see how this charge came to be formulated by carefully reading the selection from the Sermon on the Mount, as listed above.[227] When reading this selection, special attention should be given to the oft-repeated formula: "Ye have heard that it was said to them of old time ... but I say unto you ..." Perhaps we have become so accustomed to reading these and other similar passages that we fail to recognize the effect such statements must have had upon the people at the time of Jesus. When Jesus declared, "It was said ..." the people around him immediately recognized that he was referring to the law, given in ancient times through Moses. Moreover, this law was regarded by all persons as the sacred word, the final word. Therefore, any suggestion that the law should be changed or amended would be regarded by many of Jesus'

---

[225] Acts 6:14
[226] Mark 12:37
[227] Matthew 5:21-48

hearers as outright blasphemy, and an attack upon the very foundations of Judaism.

Another scripture passage from John should be read at this time.[228] This tells how an attempt was made to lead Jesus into a public declaration that the Mosaic Law should be disobeyed. Such a declaration would bring upon Jesus the condemnation of all law-abiding citizens. It would also prove that Jesus was seeking to abolish the law—as was charged against him. However, this carefully laid plot failed; and the persons who sought to discredit Jesus were themselves discredited!

The charge brought against Jesus was absolutely false. Jesus stated: "Think not that I came to destroy the law or the prophets: I came not to destroy, but to fulfil".[229] A study of the Sermon on the Mount and other similar passages shows how Jesus sought to accomplish this work of fulfillment. Jesus put new life and meaning into the various statements of the law. He showed how they were practical, workable, and how they applied to every arising situation in life. Jesus recognized that it was not enough to preserve the statements of law, as though they were rare and valuable museum pieces; they must be brought out and put into everyday use. In order to accomplish this, many of the old statements of law needed amplifying, rephrasing, and practical application. Jesus did not attempt to change principles; but he put those principles into practical use. All this is summed up by the gospel

---

[228] John 8:1-11
[229] Matthew 5:17

writer: "For the law was given through Moses; grace and truth came through Jesus Christ".[230]

Jesus was charged with violating the Sabbath law, and encouraging his followers to do likewise.
Read the passages: Mark 2:23-28; Mark 3:1-6; Luke 4:14-30; Luke 13:10-17; John 5:1-18; John 9:1-41

The above scripture passages deal with Jesus' activities on various Sabbath days, and are for the most part self-explanatory. However, these passages should now be considered in connection with the charges made against Jesus. When reading these passages, the following points should be kept well in mind:

1. Jesus was not opposed to the keeping of the Sabbath. This is shown by his actions, as recorded in Luke 4:14-30. Note especially that Jesus attended the synagogue on the Sabbath day, "as his custom was".[231]
2. So far from any intention of destroying the Sabbath, Jesus' teaching helped toward its preservation. Note how Jesus clearly stated the purpose of the Sabbath, and the basic principle upon which it rests.[232]
3. John 9:22 shows that a decision regarding Jesus and his teachings had been reached by the Jewish leaders, and that evidence was then being gathered in an effort to bring about his destruction.

---

[230] John 1:17
[231] Luke 4:16
[232] Mark 2:27

Apparently, the Jewish leaders felt that the way to preserve the Sabbath was to destroy Jesus!

In contrast with the attacks made upon Jesus because of his activities on the Sabbath, it will be well to consider briefly the metaphysical meaning of the Sabbath. The following quotation will prove helpful:

"The true Sabbath is the consciousness that we have fulfilled the divine law in both thought and act.

"The Sabbath is a very certain, definite thing. It is a state of mind that man enters or acquires when he goes into the silence, into the realm of Spirit. There he finds true rest and peace. The seventh day means the seventh or perfect stage of one's spiritual unfoldment. Man had become so lost in the darkness of sense consciousness that he could not save himself, so the Savior came. When man lays hold of the indwelling Christ, the Savior, he is raised out of the Adam consciousness into the Christ consciousness. He then enters the seventh stage of his unfoldment, where he finds sweet rest and peace."[233]

The Final Decision
Read the passages: John 11:47-57; Matt. 22:15-22; Luke 23:1-3

Having considered the threefold charges made against Jesus, we find an important question arising. Earlier in the lesson it was suggested that the underlying purpose of all these charges was to discredit the teachings of Jesus, and bring his ministry to an end. Therefore, we may now inquire: Were these charges really effective in

---

[233] Fillmore, Charles *Keep a True Lent,* p. 171

accomplishing this purpose? Did they actually bring the activities of Jesus to an end? The answer is in the negative. Undoubtedly the charges aroused heated controversy and bitter opposition, but the fact remains that the people did not rise up, as was hoped, and put an end to the ministry of Jesus. Actually, the charges seemed to increase the interest shown in Jesus' activities, and the people took sides for and against him. In other words, Jesus became the focal point of national interest; and the Jewish leaders were asking one another what else could be done to get rid of him.

The reading from John's Gospel indicates that at this point the Jewish leaders decided to take matters into their own hands. No longer would they remain behind the scenes, hoping that they might arouse the people to take action against Jesus. The leaders themselves would now do something. Accordingly, we are told of a hurriedly called meeting at which the decision was reached that Jesus' activities must now be brought to a speedy end. "So from that day forth they took counsel that they might put him to death".[234] The gospel writer calls attention to several important points:

1.   This was a combined effort made by the Sadducees and the Pharisees. As a general rule the two political parties were strongly opposed to each other; but now, what they regarded as a common danger brought them together. The Sadducee group consisted of the priests and other persons closely associated with the Temple. The High Priest was the presiding officer of the party, and the

---

[234] John 11:53

Temple was its headquarters. From what was discussed earlier in the lesson regarding Jesus' activities at the Temple, it is not difficult to understand why the Sadducees were so strongly opposed to him. The Pharisees congregated around the synagogues, and they were chiefly concerned with the ramifications of the law. Hence, the Pharisees were opposed to Jesus because of his attitude regarding the law and the Sabbath, as discussed earlier in the lesson.

2.   The Jewish leaders openly expressed their fears that Jesus' teachings and activities would lead to an insurrection, and the people would take up arms against the Romans. Such an uprising, the leaders claimed, would lead to vigorous reprisals by the Romans, who would destroy the Temple, and virtually wipe out the Jewish nation. However, the gospel writer seems to indicate that both the Sadducees and the Pharisees were more concerned for themselves and their means of livelihood than for anything that might happen to the people!

3.   This passage also indicates that the Jewish leaders took a new approach to their self-appointed task of getting rid of Jesus. Their plan now was to regard the destruction of Jesus as a national sacrifice, having as its avowed purpose the salvation of the nation. They tried to rationalize their proceedings by claiming that getting rid of Jesus would avert a national catastrophe. Moreover, this plan would also absolve the Jewish leaders from all charges of personal animosity; and

when Jesus was finally disposed of, the people would then regard them as true benefactors.

The reading from Matthew[235] tells how an effort was made to put the above-mentioned plan into operation. In this instance the idea was to trick Jesus into making a public denouncement of Roman taxation, and having him tell the people not to pay tribute to Caesar. This would be sufficient to bring about the arrest of Jesus, and his execution by the Roman authorities. However, the Scripture tells how the plan completely failed, and instead of entrapping Jesus, it brought forth a stern rebuke to Jesus' opponents. It should be noted, however, that this incident was used later against Jesus—in an altogether false way—when he was brought before Pontius Pilate just prior to the Crucifixion.[236]

Perhaps at this point we may be inclined to ask: What was Jesus' reaction to all these false charges made against him? What did he do in regard to the many attacks upon his life and ministry? Did he make a public statement, seeking to justify his teaching and activities? Or did he take some specific action, which would be recognized as a rebuttal of all that was charged against him?

In the following lesson we shall see how Jesus dealt with this difficult situation by making a complete change in his activities. The actual steps taken by Jesus will be explained in detail. For the present, however, it will suffice

---

[235] Matthew 22:15-25
[236] See Luke 23:1-3

to say that he decided to meet the "gathering storm" head-on! And this proved to be the masterstroke; for not only did it enable him to make an all-comprehensive answer to his opponents, it also enabled him later to give his followers the assuring statement, "Be of good cheer; I have overcome the world".[237]

Meanwhile, as we review the present lesson and reconsider the many controversial situations here discussed, we may be led to realize how Jesus was ever seeking to lead people into a better understanding of those old, old teachings, which had been treasured through the ages. Jesus' mission was not to "destroy" but to "fulfill." We also may attain this fulfillment as we press onward and upward with him. We may make better progress if we keep in mind James Russell Lowell's well-known lines:

"New occasions teach new duties; time makes ancient good uncouth; they must upward still, and onward, who would keep abreast of Truth."[238]

---

[237] John 16:33
[238] Lowell, James Russell *Once to Every Man and Nation*

Chapter 9 - Jesus Returns to Jerusalem

Historical Questions

1. Toward the close of his Galilean ministry, Jesus made an important decision. Explain briefly the nature of this decision, and show how it affected the Galilean ministry.

2. When Jesus was at Caesarea Philippi, he put a question to his disciples. What was this question? Also state and explain briefly the answers given by the disciples.

3. Use your own words and tell briefly what happened on the Mount of Transfiguration.

4. Why did the unnamed man bring his son to Jesus? Were the disciples able to heal the boy? What action did Jesus take when he arrived on the scene? (Mark 9:14-29)

5. What was Jesus' purpose in making his triumphal entry into Jerusalem? What was the attitude of the Jewish leaders when Jesus arrived at Jerusalem?

Metaphysical Questions

1. What does Jesus' journey from Galilee to Jerusalem represent in our consciousness? Should we regard Jerusalem as our final goal? Or is there something further to be attained?

2. From a metaphysical standpoint, how would you explain Jesus' statement: "Upon this rock I will build my church"? (Matt. 16:18)

3. List and explain briefly three important metaphysical lessons found in the story of Jesus' transfiguration.

4. An important healing miracle is recorded in Mark 9:9-29. Explain briefly why Jesus' disciples were unable to bring about the desired healing. What does this mean to us?

5. Several practical, present-day lessons are to be found in the story of Jesus' triumphal entry into Jerusalem. Mention and explain briefly three of these lessons, showing how they apply to us today.

Lesson Text
Jesus returns to Jerusalem
Read the passages: Matthew 11:20; Matthew 16:21-28; Matthew 17:22-23; Luke 13:22-35

This lesson has as its starting point an important decision made by Jesus toward the close of the period we have been considering in the past few lessons. This decision was briefly referred to in the closing section of chapter eight, and was of a twofold nature. Jesus decided that the time had arrived when he must bring his Galilean ministry to a close; and he must now return to Jerusalem, and make that city his headquarters. It will be noticed that this decision completely reversed an earlier procedure— for, in the early days of his ministry, Jesus "left Judea, and departed again into Galilee".[239] Ever since that time Jesus' activities had been centered in Galilee. However, Jesus now saw that he must go back to Jerusalem, and make his final appeal to the Jewish leaders; and the kingdom message must be presented once again in Jerusalem.

---

[239] John 4:3

When all this was accomplished, Jesus would be in a position to carry his ministry to its triumphant climax.

The Gospels show that the above-mentioned decision was closely followed by several outstanding events, all having important bearing upon Jesus' ministry. Let us, therefore, give these events careful consideration, recognizing their historical significance, and also what they mean to us.

Read the passages: Matthew 16:13-20; Mark 8:27-30; Luke 9:18-21

Caesarea Philippi is usually regarded as an important milestone or turning point in Jesus' ministry. Therefore, it will be well to make a careful study of the happenings and statements recorded in the above Scripture passages. Several details call for special attention:

Jesus' Question:
Apparently, Jesus desired to make some sort of check on the effectiveness of his Galilean ministry. He therefore put a test question to his disciples: "Who do men say that the Son of man is?" The disciples replied that, while some of the people regarded Jesus as a great man (likening him to some of the great prophets of the past), they were not yet ready to proclaim him as Messiah. This must have been somewhat of a disappointment to Jesus. However, there is a possibility that the people did not speak of Jesus as Messiah because they feared the consequences. John's Gospel states that about this time

"the Jews had agreed already, that if any man should confess him to be Christ [Messiah] he should be put out of the Synagogue".[240] Excommunication of this sort would be a serious matter! Jesus then put his question a second time, but on this occasion directing it to the disciples: "But who say ye that I am?" Peter gave immediate answer— totally disregarding the probable consequences: "Thou art the Christ [Messiah], the Son of the living God." In commending Peter for this reply, Jesus pointed out that the declaration was not made through a process of intellectual reasoning, but was a direct revelation from the Father.

"Upon this rock I will build my church"

Several explanations have been put forward regarding this statement; therefore, it should be given careful consideration. The main problem here concerns the identity of the "rock," which is to be the foundation for the church. Note the following:

1. Some persons claim that the reference is to Peter, and that Jesus' words definitely designated Peter as the foundation of the church. But had this been Jesus' intention, surely he would have made the situation clear by actually naming Peter to the position. It would have been easier (and clearer) to say: "Upon you, Peter, I will build ..." Furthermore, subsequent events reveal Peter as very unstable foundation material![241] Later in the Scriptures we read that James, brother of Jesus, not Peter, was

---

[240] John 9:22
[241] See Matthew 16:23 and Matthew 26:69-75

recognized as the presiding elder of the first church council.[242]

2. The suggestion has been made that the foundation here referred to is faith—since Peter symbolically represents faith. This is an interesting suggestion and undoubtedly has certain merits. However, it should be remembered that the symbology that designates Peter as representing faith belongs to a much later period; therefore, the name of Peter would not have this significance at the time of the conversation at Caesarea Philippi.

3. A better interpretation is arrived at by first getting clearly in mind the facts regarding the conversation. What was Jesus actually referring to when he made the statement we are now discussing? Peter had just made the declaration, "Thou art the Christ [Messiah]," and it was to this declaration that Jesus was referring. Jesus was saying, in effect: "Peter, you have spoken well for this is indeed the truth. I am the Christ; and it is upon this realization that my church must be built." The following comments will make this clear: "This reply 'Thou art the Christ, the Son of the living God' affirms two great truths concerning Jesus—his divine Sonship and his Messiahship ... but the answer of Jesus, with the play on the word petros (rock), implies that he regarded this confession of his divine Sonship and Messiahship as the

---

[242] See Acts 15

foundation upon which the new Israel of God was to be built".[243]

"This revealing Truth - 'Thou art the Christ' - direct from Spirit is the rock upon which the one and only church of Jesus Christ is built".[244]

"For other foundation can no man lay than that which is laid, which is Jesus Christ".[245]

Applying the above metaphysically, we are led to see that if we would build a Christ consciousness, the first step (or foundation) must be the realization of the indwelling Christ. We should also recognize the close relationship between the word consciousness and the word church, as used in discussing this Scripture passage. The following quotation will prove helpful:[246]

"Many have caught sight of the fact that the true church of Christ is a state of consciousness in man, but few have gone so far in the realization as to know that in the very body of each man and woman is a temple in which the Christ holds religious services at all times: 'Ye are a temple of God.' The appellation was not symbolical, but a statement of architectural truth. Under the direction of the Christ, a new body is constructed by

---

[243] *Abington Bible Commentary*, p. 980
[244] Fillmore, Charles *Talks on Truth*, p. 103
[245] I Corinthians 3:11
[246] Fillmore, *Charles Talks on Truth*, pp. 105-06

*the thinking faculty in man; the materials entering
into this superior structure are the spiritualized
organic substances, and the new creation is the
temple or body of Spirit. It breathes an atmosphere
and is thrilled with a life energy more real than that
of the external form. When one who has come into
the church of Christ feels the stirring within him of
this body of the Spirit, he knows what Paul meant
when he said, 'There is a natural body, there is also
a spiritual body'*

"I will give thee the keys ..."

Note that the statement regarding the "keys" as
related to this conversation, appears only in Matthew. The
accounts in Mark and Luke omit this section. However, it
should be further noted that while this statement is
reported as being addressed to Peter in the conversation
at Caesarea Philippi, the same words were spoken to all
the other disciples on other occasions.[247] These references
clearly indicate that the "power of the keys" was not
intended to be limited to Peter.

We may ask, then: What are these "keys"? The
following quotation should prove helpful:[248]

*"The 'keys' to this 'kingdom of heaven' are in
binding (affirmations) and loosing (denials). ... All
affirmations and denials made by man from this
plane of consciousness control the realm of free
ideas or heavens ... This is especially true of bodily*

---

[247] Compare Matt. 16:19 with Matt. 18:18 and John 20:23.
[248] *Metaphysical Bible Dictionary*, pp. 516-17 - Peter

conditions. If you allow Peter to speak of erroneous states of consciousness as true conditions, you will be bound to them and you will suffer; but if you see to it that he pronounces them free from errors of sense, they will be 'loosed'.

In other words, our attitude of mind today determines what will be the condition of our body and affairs tomorrow!

"Tell no man."

Many readers of the Gospels are puzzled in regard to this statement. Why should Jesus charge his disciples "that they should tell no man that be was the Christ"? Several possible reasons may be suggested:

1. Protection for the disciples. As mentioned above, open confession regarding the Messiahship of Jesus would result in excommunication; and this would work hardship on all persons concerned.
2. To openly proclaim Jesus as the long-awaited Messiah might lead to an uprising of the Jews against the Romans—something which Jesus, thus far, had sought to guard against.
3. Possibly the most important reason for the enjoined secrecy is to be found in the fact that the recognition of the Christ is an individual matter, and each person must make the discovery for himself. The difference between Peter and the other disciples, as shown in the

story, is similar to the differences between people today. The individual revelation came to Peter; and this revelation from "the Father" must likewise come to us as individuals.

The Transfiguration

Read the passages: Matthew 17:1-13; Mark 9:2-8; Luke 9: 28-36

The story of Jesus' transfiguration is so well known that only brief comments are necessary. However, the Scripture passages given above should be carefully read and compared. The important point is to recognize that Jesus was facing a very serious situation; consequently, his actions should be regarded as containing some important lessons. It would be well at this point to refer back to Lesson Seven, and reread the comments regarding Jesus' teaching through actions. Note the following important details:

1. Jesus ascended the mountain for the purpose of intensive prayer. Luke brings this out very clearly and also indicates some results of Jesus' prayer activities.
2. Jesus took with him three disciples—Peter, John, and James. Metaphysically, this indicates that prayer should have within it the qualities of faith, love, and wisdom.
3. The Gospel writer states that "as he [Jesus] was praying, the fashion of his countenance was altered ..." This may remind us of the familiar statement, "Prayer changes things." However, we should

amplify this statement, somewhat in this way: "Prayer changes things, because prayer first changes us." In other words, outer things or conditions are transformed, because there has first been a transformation within ourselves.

4. The appearance of Moses and Elijah indicates that The Law and the Prophets" (Hebrew teaching) find fulfillment in Jesus. Several well-known Scripture passages throw additional light on this happening: "And beginning from Moses and from all the prophets, he [Jesus] interpreted to them in all the scriptures the things concerning himself".[249] "For the law was given through Moses: grace and truth came through Jesus Christ".[250]

5. The message of divine approval: "This is my Son, my chosen: hear ye him".[251] This is similar to the message given immediately following Jesus' baptism.[252] It should be noted that in both instances Jesus had made an important decision, and his decision received confirmation and divine approval. Does not this inner voice also speak to us? "The Spirit himself bears witness with our spirit, that we are children of God".[253]

6. Note the contrast between Peter's expressed desire to remain on the mountaintop, and Jesus' action in making immediate return to the valley. This may mean that moments of spiritual exaltation

---

[249] Luke 24:27
[250] John 1:17
[251] Luke 9:35
[252] See Matthew 3:17
[253] Romans 8:16

are intended, not as an end in themselves, but as a preparation for further spiritual activities. Mountaintop experiences are for illumination and inspiration, so that we may be filled with new strength and courage to take up the tasks that await us in the valley.

Something akin to Jesus Christ's transfiguration may occur in our life experience from time to time. Following an important decision that sends us onward and upward along the path of spiritual unfoldment, there may come to us a period of great uplift, or spiritual exaltation. We may feel that we are nearer to God than we have ever been before. We seem to reach the high point in spiritual experience, for with Jesus Christ we have ascended the Mount of Transfiguration.

Healing the Demented Boy
Read the passages: Matthew 17:9-21; Mark 9:9-29; Luke 9:37-45

The Gospel writers place this healing miracle immediately following Jesus' transfiguration, and the connection is readily recognized. Peter expressed the desire to remain on the mountaintop, but Jesus was aware that important work awaited him in the valley. The significance of this was discussed earlier in the lesson, but several other features also call for careful consideration.
1. The appeal for help:
   The Scripture passages given above explain how an unnamed man brought his son to Jesus for healing.

Jesus had gone away to the mountain to pray, taking with him Peter, John, and James. Evidently, the man was deeply disappointed in not being able to contact Jesus. However, several of the disciples still remained at the camping point, and the man appealed to them for the needed help. But the appeal brought only further disappointment, for these disciples were unable to heal the demented boy.

2. The failure of the disciples:
    This failure is rather difficult to understand. At an earlier period Jesus had given his disciples instructions and had empowered them to do healing work.[254] Furthermore, the Gospels indicate that the disciples actually accomplished healing work, even when Jesus was not present.[255] Why, then, should they fail on this occasion?

3. There are several possible explanations, some of which will be mentioned later. But there is also an important metaphysical lesson to be recognized here. Note that Peter, John, and James were not present —being away with Jesus on the mountain. It should also be remembered that these disciples symbolize faith, love, and wisdom. This section of the story, therefore, may be regarded as emphasizing the need of faith, love, and wisdom in all our healing work. Without faith, love, and wisdom, all of our attempts to bring about healing are likely to fail.

---

[254] See Matthew 10:1
[255] See Luke 10:17

4. The attitude of Jesus:

   Many Bible readers find the conversation between
   Jesus and this unnamed man somewhat puzzling;
   and because of this, the really important point in
   this passage is frequently overlooked. Therefore, in
   order to make the situation clear, let us paraphrase
   the conversation using present-day language, in
   this way:

   *The Man: "Rabbi, I brought my son to you, hoping
   that you could cast out the evil spirit that threatens
   to destroy him; but you had gone away."*
   *Jesus: "Yes, I had gone to yonder mountain, to
   pray."*
   *The Man: "But some of your disciples were standing
   nearby, and I appealed to them for healing help.
   They spoke some words, and laid their hands on my
   son's head; but he was not healed."*
   *Jesus: "I certainly regret that my disciples were
   unable to help you."*
   *The Man: "But Rabbi, now that you are returned, if
   you are really able to do anything, will you heal my
   son?"*
   *Jesus: "My friend, I want you to know that this
   word 'if,' which you use so freely, does not apply to
   me, but to yourself! This is not a question of 'if I am
   able to do anything'; but, rather, 'if you are able to
   believe.' There can be no doubt about my power to
   heal—for this has been demonstrated again and
   again—but there does appear to be some doubt
   about your ability to believe. Surely you remember*

the saying: 'All things are possible to him that
believeth.'
The Man: "Forgive me, Rabbi! I do believe in you —
or, at least, I have been trying to believe. But I see
now that there must be something lacking; so help
me to believe as I ought! Help me to understand
what belief really means."

A glance at the Scripture passage will show that immediately following this conversation Jesus spoke the healing word, and the boy was healed.

An Important "Postscript"

Further discussing the apparent failure of the disciples, the story tells how, later in the day, the disciples asked Jesus: "How is it that we could not cast it [the evil spirit] out?" And Jesus replied: "This kind can come out by nothing, save by prayer [and fasting]."[256] Two things should be noted in regard to this reply:

1. The disciples must have felt somewhat crestfallen at that time, on account of their failure. But Jesus did not upbraid them for their lack of faith, or any other contributing cause. Rather, his reply was calculated to "spare their feelings," as the saying goes. This is another indication of Jesus' regard for his disciples.
2. There is also an important lesson here: We have already seen that healing work calls for faith, love, and wisdom. However, further emphasis is now placed on the necessity for "prayer and fasting"— which may be

---

[256] Mark 9:29

interpreted in terms of affirmation and denial. We usually think of healing as being a restoration; but before such restoration can take place there must be a casting out of all negative influences, such as hinder the work of healing. Hence, the emphasis upon "prayer and fasting." In other words, the casting out is accomplished through denial and affirmation.

The Triumphal Entry

Read the passages: Matthew 21:1-11; Mark 11:1-11; Luke 19:29-44; John 12:12-19; Luke 9:51-62

Jesus' triumphal return to Jerusalem, on what we now term "Palm Sunday," is recorded in all four Gospels. This indicates that the Gospel writers regarded the event as being of great importance. Therefore, it will be well to read carefully all four accounts, noting the main points and also any variations.

After reading the story, as suggested, we may ask: What was the actual meaning and purpose of this triumphal entry? Why did Jesus return to Jerusalem in this manner?

We readily recognize that the recorded happenings represent something more than a spontaneous outburst of popular enthusiasm. A careful reading of the above Scripture passages reveals that Jesus had carefully planned certain happenings connected with this entry. Note how he had previously arranged with certain persons for the loan of a donkey, and the precautions taken to insure that these arrangements were properly carried out.[257] It should be noted further that this is the only Christian Scriptural reference to Jesus using this form of transportation. Apparently, on all other occasions Jesus and his disciples made their journeys on foot. Why, then, did Jesus make this special arrangement at this time?

It would seem that in this triumphal entry Jesus was making a final presentation of his teaching regarding the coming of the Messiah. Throughout his ministry Jesus sought to correct popular misunderstandings in this regard, and several references have been made to this in earlier lessons. But now Jesus saw that time was running out. He therefore decided to make what may be termed a "pictorial presentation," or to present an "acted parable," as a final effort to help the people to understand. What Jesus was seeking to do can be understood best by reading the following passage from the Hebrew Scriptures:[258]

> *"Rejoice greatly, O daughter of Zion; shout, O daughter of Jerusalem: behold, thy king cometh unto thee; he is just, and having salvation; lowly, and riding upon an ass, even a colt the foal of an ass. And I will cut off the chariot from Ephraim, and the horse from Jerusalem; and the battle bow shall be cut off; and he shall speak peace unto the nations: and his dominion shall be from sea to sea, and from the River to the ends of the earth"*

---

[257] See Mark 11:2-7
[258] Zechariah 9:9-10

Seeking to understand this Scripture passage, we should recall that when these words were first written, an enemy was invading the kingdom. The people cried out for a deliverer—a king who would be strong enough to overthrow the enemy and lead his people to victory, just as David did in ancient times. However, the prophet here presents a different type of deliverer. The new king would not be a military leader, riding upon a horse (symbol of war), but would come "lowly, and riding upon an ass." In other words, this king would recognize that force was not to be overthrown by more force, but by love; and that deliverance would come, not by the power of man, but by the power of God. "Not by might, nor by power, but by my Spirit, says Jehovah of hosts".[259] And was not this the very picture that Jesus was seeking to present to the people in his triumphal entry? He was saying, in effect: "This is how the Messiah comes, just as the ancient prophet declared. So why not recognize that the Messiah and his Kingdom are now truly at hand? This is what I have been seeking to teach. Why not accept your good, now?"

However, the story of the triumphal entry has a tragic ending. Notwithstanding the popular acclaim, the Jewish leaders refused to acknowledge Jesus as Messiah, and they continued in their efforts to bring about his destruction. We see something of Jesus' reaction to this rejection in his sorrowful statement: "You know not the time of thy visitation".[260]

Metaphysically interpreted, Jesus' journey from Galilee to Jerusalem may be seen as a symbol of the

---

[259] Zechariah 4:6
[260] Luke 19:44

journey we also must undertake as we advance from sense consciousness or mortal consciousness to spiritual consciousness. Like Jesus, we first make the great decision as at Caesarea Philippi; and this may be followed by an experience of spiritual exaltation and illumination as at the Transfiguration. Then we proceed toward our Jerusalem—representing the realization that we live, and move, and have our being in God, and the experience of his abiding peace. If we make a careful analysis of Jesus' journey, we shall readily see how several outstanding features also apply to our journey. Note the following:

1. At the start—a set purpose:

    At this point it will be well to reread Luke 9: 51-62, as mentioned above. (It should be noted that this passage really has reference to Jesus' journey from Galilee to Jerusalem, but for some reason it has been placed a little earlier in Luke's Gospel.) However, the important point in this passage is the emphasis placed on Jesus' unwavering determination to carry through his plan of going to Jerusalem: "He stedfastly set his face to go to Jerusalem." Note also Jesus' words to those who would follow him on his journey. There must be no misunder-standing, no wavering, no turning back! "No man, having put his hand to the plow, and looking back, is fit for the kingdom of God".[261]

    Surely all this applies to our projected journey. Having once started, we must press steadily forward, resisting everything that would turn us aside, and keeping our face set toward our

---

[261] Luke 9:62

Jerusalem. "Forgetting the things which are behind ... I press on toward the goal, unto the prize of the high calling of God in Christ Jesus".[262]

2. On the way—a symbolic action:
    The Gospel account states that Jesus came riding on an ass "whereon no man ever yet sat".[263] Jesus therefore undertook to ride to Jerusalem using an unbroken and unsaddled donkey—truly a difficult task! Indeed, this performance might well be classified as a miracle, and bracketed with Jesus' earlier miracle of stilling the storm. Yet Jesus was in complete control and rode evenly and safely. Metaphysically, this indicates that if we are to undertake our spiritual journey, as suggested above, one of our early activities must be to bring our physical powers under control. We must say in regard to our entire being—spirit, soul, body— "Christ is in control!"

3. Arrival—and a seeming setback:
    At first reading, the story of the triumphal entry seems to end in a rather tragic way, as already indicated. Jesus' arrival at Jerusalem is depicted in the Gospels as somewhat of an anti-climax. The people along the wayside had been greeting Jesus with loud acclaim; but on his arrival at Jerusalem the Jewish leaders and city officials completely ignored him. Apparently, then, Jesus' pictorial presentation had been in vain; for although loud cries of "Hosanna!" had been heard, Jesus was not

---

[262] Philippians 3:13-14
[263] Mark 11:2

publicly acknowledged as the Messiah. However, later events showed that this seeming setback was in reality the time for a fresh beginning. Jesus, having made this presentation, was then able to enter upon the final period of his ministry, with its triumphant conclusion.

All this has an important lesson for us: In our spiritual development we should always regard seeming setbacks as points of new beginning. What may appear to be failure is, in reality, only a breathing space, where we may gather fresh energy and enthusiasm to press forward to higher attainments. Moreover, in all our spiritual experiences we are following in the footsteps of Jesus; and with him we should regard our arrival at Jerusalem as a fresh starting point for the further experiences of Holy Week. It must have been a situation such as this that the writer of the Epistle to the Hebrews had in mind, when he wrote:[264]

> "Therefore let us also, seeing we are compassed about with so great a cloud of witnesses, lay aside every weight, and the sin which doth so easily beset us, and run with patience the race that is set before us, looking unto Jesus the author and perfector of our faith, who for the joy that was set before him endured the cross, despising shame, and hath sat down at the right hand of the throne of God".

---

[264] Hebrews 12:1-2

Chapter 10 - Important Happenings in Jerusalem

Historical Questions

1. In your own words describe briefly the anointing of Jesus by Mary. Mention the objections made by some bystanders, and state how Jesus replied to them.

2. Explain briefly why certain Greeks sought an interview with Jesus. What suggestions were probably made at that time? How did Jesus deal with these suggestions?

3. When Jesus washed the feet of His disciples, what special request was made by Peter? How would you interpret Jesus' reply?

4. Why did Jesus' opponents seek to arrest Him secretly? Explain briefly what may have been Judas' purpose in helping to bring about this arrest.

5. When and where did Jesus institute what we now term "The Lord's Supper" or "Holy Communion"? Tell briefly what took place in the Upper Room at that time. In your answer make clear the difference between the "Passover" and "The Lord's Supper."

Metaphysical Questions

1. Mention (and explain briefly) an important metaphysical lesson arising out of the story of the anointing of Jesus by Mary.

2. Explain briefly how the conversation between Jesus and the Greeks may help us to stand firm in regard to our ideals and high purposes.

3. What is indicated metaphysically by the story of the foot-washing? Explain briefly why such a cleansing is necessary. Also mention how Jesus' action may affect our attitudes regarding certain types of service.

4. What does Judas represent in consciousness? In what way or ways may the Judas activity affect our spiritual development? Name the apostle who later replaced Judas. What is the meaning of this name?

5. What is represented by the bread and wine used in Holy Communion? How do we partake of these in a spiritual manner? How does Holy Communion help in our spiritual development?

Lesson Text

Read the passages: Matthew 16:21-28; Mark 10:32-45

This lesson deals with what is usually termed the closing phase of Jesus' ministry. From the standpoint of time, this covers only a very brief period. Nevertheless, during this period there were quite a number of important happenings; and these should be given very careful consideration. Several of these happenings will be discussed in this lesson, while others will have a place in the lesson that follows. However, if we are to grasp the full significance of these happenings, it will be necessary to review briefly some of Jesus' activities up to this point.

First, we should recall that the main purpose of Jesus' ministry was to lead people into the kingdom of God. Jesus proclaimed that this kingdom was "at hand",[265] and "in the midst of you";[266] but he also recognized that something in addition to this proclamation was necessary. Somehow the people must be brought into the kingdom, so that they might experience the "life abundant" and participate in all the blessings prepared for them "from the foundation of the world."[267] Jesus, therefore, sought in every way possible to lead people into the kingdom; and the Gospels indicate how Jesus in his ministry took several well-defined steps to accomplish this important work. Note the following:

Activities During the Early Judean Ministry

During this short period, Jesus taught daily in the Temple courts, having as his main theme "the kingdom." Just what Jesus was seeking to accomplish is clearly shown in his conversation with Nicodemus.[268] But Jesus found that the people were not responding to his kingdom message; therefore, he decided to make a change in his plans—leaving Jerusalem and Judea and journeying northward into Galilee.

Activities during the Galilean Ministry.

Jesus' Galilean ministry covered a period of more than two years. During this time Jesus presented his

---

[265] Mark 1:15
[266] Luke 17:20
[267] See John 10:10 and Matthew 25:34
[268] See John 3:1-22

teaching in many varied ways and made great efforts to lead people into the kingdom. But, as in the case of the Judean ministry, the results were disappointing. People listened to Jesus' teaching, but they did not acknowledge him as Messiah, nor did they seek entrance into the kingdom. Jesus therefore decided that an entirely different type of effort was necessary—and this brings us to his third step.

The Return to Jerusalem.
    In chapter nine a question was raised as to why Jesus decided to bring his Galilean ministry to a close and return to Jerusalem; several possibilities were suggested. However, following this brief review, we are now able to recognize the basic reason for the change. Jesus saw that both the Judean and the Galilean ministries had not produced the desired response from the people, and therefore he must now undertake a work of entirely different nature. In other words, since Plan One and Plan Two had not proved successful, Plan Three must now be put into operation. Jesus decided that instead of continuing to present the kingdom message through the forms of teaching employed thus far, he would now make the presentation through his own person; and such a presentation would surely open the way for all persons to attain "abundant entrance" into the kingdom. Earlier in his ministry, Jesus said: "If any man would come after me, let him deny himself, and take up his cross, and follow me".[269] Now Jesus decided to lead the march into the kingdom personally, and to press forward to the culmination of his

---

[269] Mark 8:34

ministry, even though this meant that he must needs journey by way of the Cross. The following statement by Jesus is significant:[270]

> *And he [Jesus] took unto him the twelve, and said unto them, Behold, we go up to Jerusalem, and all the things that are written through the prophets shall be accomplished unto the Son of man. For he shall be delivered up to the Gentiles, and shall be mocked, and shamefully treated, and spit upon: and they shall scourge him and kill him: and on the third day he shall rise again.*

Thus, having Jesus' purpose clearly before us, we are now in a better position to understand his activities during this closing period of his ministry at Jerusalem. The following important happenings should be carefully studied.

The Anointing
Read the passage: John 12:1-8. (Compare with Matthew 26:6-13; Mark 14:3-9; Luke 7:36-50.)

While this anointing activity cannot be actually classified as one of the "happenings in Jerusalem," it does have an important place in the closing phase of Jesus' ministry. Hence, it will be well to read and carefully check the passages listed above. The first thing to be settled is this: Should we think of these Scripture passages as reports of several happenings of similar nature, or should

---

[270] Luke 18:31-33

we see here only one happening, variously reported? Certainly there are a number of differences in the accounts, and some of these differences are very pronounced. For example: John's account states that Mary, the sister of Lazarus, made the anointing; the other accounts make mention of "a woman," and "a woman ... who was a sinner"—and such terms would scarcely apply to Mary of Bethany! Traditionally, Mary Magdalene has been long associated with this anointing, and the terms mentioned might easily refer to her. Probably this tradition arose from the fact that Luke mentions Mary Magdalene immediately following his account of the anointing.[271] However, despite the differences mentioned, all the Scripture passages contain substantially the same story, and it will be noted that the similarities more than outweigh the differences. Therefore, for purposes of study, we may regard this as one happening.

At this point, two important questions arise:

What was the actual purpose of this anointing?

At first reading this appears to be a loving, gracious act, performed for the purpose of expressing the woman's sincere devotion to Jesus. Undoubtedly, this devotional aspect should be recognized. However, it should also be recalled that the word Messiah (or Christ) actually means "The Anointed One," and there are many Old Testament references to this process of anointing. It seems possible, therefore, that through this act of anointing, the woman was symbolically acknowledging Jesus as the Messiah. She could not speak the word openly, because the Jewish

---

[271] See Luke 8:2

authorities had forbidden anyone to refer to Jesus as the Messiah, imposing heavy penalties upon transgressors.[272] But it would seem that the woman skillfully bypassed this prohibitive regulation, and through her loving action she proclaimed that Jesus was indeed the "Anointed One," the Messiah! Apparently Jesus fully recognized the purpose of this anointing, for not only did he speak a word of approval, but he also stated that this story would be told "Where ever the gospel shall be preached throughout the whole world".[273]

Why did Jesus make reference to his "burial"?

In the accounts of the anointing, it will be noticed that the Gospel writers report Jesus as connecting the event with his forthcoming death and burial. This must have been very mystifying to all persons present, since Jesus was then a comparatively young man, with the possibility of many years of active life before him. Why, then, should he speak of his burial? The answer is to be found in the fact that, at that time, Jesus had charted his course for the final effort in his ministry, as discussed earlier in this lesson. Jesus was fully aware of what awaited him at Jerusalem, and was prepared to lay down his life for the kingdom. In this connection, it is significant to note (assuming the anointing was performed by Mary Magdalene, as tradition avers) that Mary was the first to visit the tomb of Jesus on Easter morning.[274] Mary's purpose in visiting the tomb was to anoint Jesus' body—

---

[272] See John 9:22
[273] Mark 14:9
[274] John 20: 1-18

probably with the remaining portion of the costly perfume, left over from the first anointing; and as a reward for this expression of love, Mary Magdalene was the first person to greet the risen Lord on the morning of the Resurrection.

Seeking metaphysical interpretation for this anointing activity, we readily recognize the "precious ointment" as a symbol of love. As the story opens, mention is made of the ointment being contained in an alabaster cruse; and had it remained there, nothing worthwhile would have been accomplished. But the Gospel writers tell how Mary broke open the cruse and poured some of the perfumed ointment upon the head and feet of Jesus. Mary thus released the soothing fragrance and healing qualities of the ointment, imparting a blessing to her Lord, and filling the house with rich perfume. In a somewhat similar way, love abiding in our heart may be designated as "precious" and be highly esteemed, but this is not sufficient. Only as love is actually poured out upon persons and situations does it impart its blessings to those concerned. Love was not meant to be hoarded within the heart. If good is to be accomplished, and if situations are to be transformed, we must break the "alabaster cruse" and start pouring out this "precious ointment" of love.

Visit of the "Greeks"
Read the passage: John 12:20-36

This visit is recorded only in John's Gospel, and so many readers find the account somewhat puzzling. The tendency, therefore, is to sidetrack study of this happening and press forward to the stirring events ahead. However, what took place during this visit had an important bearing on the closing phase of Jesus' ministry, so it will be well to trace carefully the sequence of events. Apparently, the Gospel writer omitted several details, and these omissions are the main cause of the difficulties suggested above. But a close study of the context will reveal the substance of these omissions and enable us to straighten out some of the puzzling features of this story, which will then read somewhat as follows:

Several Greek-speaking Jews, probably coming from the northern section of the Holy Land, were visiting Jerusalem and had been taking part in some religious observances. These visitors seemed to have a special interest in Jesus and apparently desired to warn him of his perilous position. They told Jesus that the Jewish leaders were about to arrest him and put him to death, and they urged him to make an immediate return to Galilee. Jesus then informed these kindly-disposed visitors that he was fully aware of the danger, and, indeed, that this was his very purpose in coming to Jerusalem. He said, "The hour is come, that the Son of man should be glorified."

At this point the visitors, and probably some of the disciples, raised the question: "But how do you know that such a sacrifice is in accord with the divine purpose?" Instead of answering directly, Jesus looked to God in prayer, and the answer came in a most unexpected manner. People standing nearby said that a storm was approaching, for there was a sound like thunder. Other persons said that an angel had spoken to Jesus. But Jesus declared that this was God's answer to the prayer he had uttered, and that this signified divine approval of the work he was about to undertake. Jesus also stated that the answer came in this way, "not for my sake, but for your [the bystanders'] sakes." Here it should be noted that Jesus made a similar statement in connection with his prayer at the grave of Lazarus.[275] Following this prayer and answer, Jesus restated his purpose in coming to Jerusalem—and it is here that we see the importance of this happening. Jesus declared again that "the Son of man must be lifted up," so that through the mighty work he was about to accomplish, the way would be opened into the kingdom.

The present-day meaning of this story is very important. There are times in our experience when well-meaning friends or external conditions may tend to divert us from our God-given objectives. We may be inclined to take a second look at what the Christian Scriptures term "the high calling of God in Christ Jesus",[276] and try to convince ourselves that to settle for something on a lower plane might be the way of wisdom. Many similar situations may arise. But at such times, a rereading of the Scripture passage now before us will remind us how Jesus went forward unwaveringly to complete his divinely-appointed mission, not allowing any possibilities of lesser good to divert him; and then we may hear him say to us: "Go thou, and do likewise."

---

[275] See John 11:42
[276] Philippians 3:14

Jesus' Parables of Urgent Appeal.

During the closing phase of his ministry, Jesus presented several important parables to his hearers. These parables were listed in an earlier lesson under the heading "Parables of Urgent Appeal," and these should now be reread. The references are as follows:

1. The Two Sons: Matthew 21:28-32
2. The Wicked Husbandmen: Matthew 21:33-46
3. The Wedding Feast: Matthew 22:1-14
4. The Ten Virgins: Matthew 25:1-13
5. The Talents: Matthew 25:14-30
6. The Pounds: Luke 19:11-28

In these parables we find Jesus earnestly pleading with the people—especially the Jewish leaders— to change their ways of thinking and living, so that they might share in the joys of the kingdom. These parables differ from those given during the earlier periods of Jesus' ministry, in that they contain a marked note of urgency. The time for definite action was indeed "at hand," and some decisions had to be made and actions taken without further delay. These parables represent Jesus' final appeal to his hearers.

The Foot-Washing

Read the passage: John 13:1-20

The story of Jesus washing the feet of the disciples is closely associated with the closing phase of his ministry, and most of the details are well known. However, there is one rather puzzling problem connected with this happening, and this should be given careful consideration. You will notice that this story is given only in John's Gospel. It is also apparent that John regarded this happening as highly important, since he gives a carefully detailed description of what took place. Why, then, is this story not given in the Gospels of Matthew, Mark, and Luke? What reasons would the synoptic writers have for omitting such a unique event?

Of course, there are several other instances where actions of Jesus are recorded in only one Gospel, and you will encounter these from time to time. In most cases, reasons for omission are easily recognized. But the foot-washing story seems to be in an entirely different category, and there must have been some special reason (or reasons) for omitting such an important happening. This reason becomes apparent when we recall that the main purpose of the synoptic Gospels was to proclaim and emphasize the Messiahship of Jesus. When these Gospels were written, the messianic controversy was at its height. Christian converts were taught that Jesus was indeed the long-expected Messiah, but many Jewish leaders continued to denounce him as an impostor. Under such circumstances, therefore, the synoptists probably recognized that the foot-washing story would tend to nullify their teachings regarding the Messiahship of Jesus; for it was unthinkable that the Messiah would undertake such a menial task as this. Foot-washing was a task for a slave, not a Messiah! Therefore, while this story may have been known to the synoptic writers, they apparently decided that their purpose would best be served by omitting it from their Gospels.

But a further question arises: If the above reasoning is correct, how did the story find a place in John's Gospel? Would not the same objections apply there also?

Seeking to answer this question, we should recall that John's Gospel is placed among the later writings in the Christian Scriptures, and the actual date of writing may have been as late as 120 CE. By this time much of the controversy regarding Jesus had subsided, and his place as Messiah was firmly established in the Early Church. Furthermore, the number of Gentiles in the church had greatly increased, and these would not have been influenced by the objections of the Jewish leaders. Therefore, the story of the foot-washing may have been more acceptable to readers of John's Gospel than to the earlier readers of the synoptic Gospels. There are also indications that John had a special reason for including the story of the foot-washing in his Gospel. At the time of writing, John was called upon to meet certain tendencies which had arisen within the Early Church, and this story seemed to have special application to this situation. Consider the following:

At the time when John's Gospel was written all the apostles (with the exception of John) had passed away, and a new generation of Christian leaders had arisen. The church had also greatly increased in numbers. But it would appear that there was a tendency among some of the new leaders to regard themselves as persons of high importance and to act in a haughty manner toward their fellow Christians. Long before this, the Apostle Paul had stated that a Christian should not "think of himself more highly than he ought to think";[277] and he also wrote, "I beseech you to walk worthily of the calling wherewith ye are called, with all lowliness and meekness".[278] Apparently all of this good advice had been forgotten; and it would seem that John decided to include the story of the foot-washing in his Gospel in the hope that it would be received as a timely lesson in humility. If Jesus could so humble himself, surely his followers might be expected to do likewise!

There is also a possibility that the story of the foot-washing was included in John's Gospel to help offset certain teachings which were then creeping into the Early Church. The situation will be better understood if we recall that the church at Ephesus, where the Gospel of John was written, was founded by the Apostle Paul.[279] Paul also founded many other church groups in the surrounding area. But just prior to the time when John's Gospel was written, some Christian teachers were placing emphasis upon what was later termed "the primacy of Peter." They claimed that Peter was the chief apostle, and that his power and authority had been passed along to his designated successors. The story of the foot-washing would tend to nullify all such claims. In the story, Peter is pictured as seeking some sort of preeminence over the other disciples, for he said, "Not my feet only [like the

_____

[277] Romans 12:3
[278] Ephesians 4:1-2
[279] See Acts 19

other disciples], but also my hands and my head".[280] Jesus, however, rebuked Peter and, to use a familiar phrase, set him in his proper place. Jesus indicated that there was to be no preeminence in this matter, but that what he was doing would apply equally to all the disciples. Thus we have in this story not only an important lesson in humility, but also a helpful setting straight of the record.

For us today, the story of the foot-washing has an important metaphysical meaning, since it symbolically indicates the necessity for cleansing the understanding. The importance of this cleansing is shown by the frequent misunderstandings arising among the present-day followers of Jesus— similar to the misunderstandings that arose among his disciples long ago. The following quotation will prove helpful when studying this story: [281]

> *"By washing the feet of his disciples Jesus denied the race idea of matter as all-important and taught the value of service. Even Peter (spiritual faith) had to be cleansed of his belief in the seeming reality of material conditions. ... As through his great love Christ cleansed our understanding, we should cleanse the understanding of our fellows. He delegates to his disciples the power to cleanse man's mind of false standards of life".*

It will also be noted that in this foot-washing activity Jesus placed a new dignity on all forms of service, no matter how humble the service might be. He said, "For

---

[280] John 13:9
[281] Fillmore, Charles *Mysteries of John* pp. 126-27

I have given you an example that ye should do as I have
done to you." In a somewhat similar statement, given in
Luke 22:24-27, Jesus intimated that greatness is to be
measured in terms of service; and then he added, "I am
among you as he that serves."

The Enigma of Judas

Read the passages: Matthew 26:14-16; Luke 17:1-2 and
22:3-6; John 13:21-30; Mark 14:43-50; John 18:1-11;
Matthew 27:3-10; Acts 1:15-26.

In Scriptural study, questions often arise
concerning Judas Iscariot, the betrayer of Jesus. What
should we think about Judas? What sort of man was he?
What part did he actually play in Jesus' ministry? The
Scriptures label Judas as "a thief" and "a devil"; but some
early writers claimed that Judas had attained a higher
degree of spiritual enlightenment than his fellow apostles.
In modern times, appraisals of Judas range all the way
from "a sincere but mistaken man" to "an out-and-out
villain, the perpetrator of the blackest crime in history."
What, then, are we to think of Judas? Where should we
place him in the closing phase of Jesus' ministry?

Perhaps the best method of procedure will be to
gather some important facts regarding Judas as recorded
in the Christian Scriptures and give these careful
consideration. Several helpful passages along these lines
are listed above. Then we may place alongside these facts
some reasonable possibilities regarding the motivating
thoughts and the activities of Judas. This will give meaning
to the facts and enable us to enter into a better

understanding of the entire situation. This would work out somewhat as follows:

1. Judas Iscariot: Some books of reference explain the surname as meaning "belonging to Kerioth," a city in Moab territory; but here it should be noted that Judas is usually regarded as being a Judean. The further suggestion has been made that the word Iscariot may have reference to the political leanings of Judas—something similar to "Simon, the Zealot." This would indicate that Judas was an ardent patriot, probably associated with an insurrectionist organization, and that his messianic hopes would include the complete overthrow of Rome.

2. Judas' conference with the priests: The point to be recognized here is that the Jewish leaders desired to arrest Jesus, but dared not do so publicly. At that time Jesus had many followers, and a public arrest might easily have led to a riot—something that the leaders sought to avoid. Judas, therefore, went to the priests to inform them that he could bring about the arrest of Jesus in a private way, without danger of a riot; and for this piece of work he was to be paid a certain sum of money. The "thirty pieces of silver" may have represented what we would term a down payment to make this a legal contract.

3. But why did Judas desire to bring about the arrest of Jesus? There was no personal animosity; neither was money the consideration. The answer seems to be that Judas believed such an arrest would

force Jesus to declare himself as the Messiah—first miraculously freeing himself, and then starting on the work of freeing the Jewish nation from Roman bondage. In this connection, it should be noted that Judas had no special love for the priests, nor did he desire to see them successful in their attempts to arrest Jesus. Indeed, Judas apparently believed that when Jesus declared himself as the Messiah, the priests would experience feelings of deep chagrin, and they would also be money out of pocket! However, if this was actually the plan of Judas, he was doomed to disappointment; for when Jesus was finally arrested there was no resistance, and he was led quietly away to trial and condemnation. The bitter repentance and tragic death of Judas seem to indicate that the possibility of failure, or personal injury to Jesus, had not entered his mind. Matthew reports that Judas, in his bitter grief, committed suicide; but Luke indicates that this was "accidental death."

4. Jesus' attitude toward Judas: The Scriptures make it clear that Jesus was fully aware of the activities of Judas, although he made no effort to restrain the betrayer nor did he condemn him for this traitorous behavior. Jesus took a compassionate attitude toward Judas—having in mind the forthcoming verdict of history; but he allowed Judas to take his own course. What would be the explanation of such an attitude? It seems clear that Jesus came to Jerusalem fully recognizing what the outcome would be, and he was prepared to make

the supreme sacrifice. Possibly Jesus saw the action of Judas as fitting into this final plan, and he accepted it accordingly. Perhaps Jesus also saw that this was the only way really to help Judas; for only after Judas actually put his plan into operation was he led to realize how erroneous his way of thinking was.

5. Metaphysical significance: Judas is usually regarded as symbolizing the life forces within us in their unredeemed state. Judas acted as treasurer for the early organization formed by Jesus and his disciples. Similarly, Judas in consciousness acts as the custodian of those life forces, powers, and abilities that God has bestowed upon us. But what about the use of these powers, forces, and abilities? Should they be used to further personal plans, or should they be used according to divine direction? The Judas within us seeks to betray us into misusing what God has given, emphasizing the personal side, and seeking satisfaction for self. Judas claims that "the end justifies the means," and his prayer is: "My will, not thine, be done!" It is significant that, following the death of Judas, his place as an apostle was given to Matthias—whose name means "wholly given to Jehovah."

"In Remembrance of Me"

Read the passages: Matthew 26:17-35; Mark 14:12-31; Luke 22:7-23; John 13:1-14; I Cor. 11: 17-34

The passages listed above explain how and when Jesus instituted what we now term "The Lord's Supper" or "Holy Communion." In these passages the Gospel writers set ajar the doors of the Upper Room and give us a brief glimpse of the important events taking place therein. Surely, we stand on holy ground! The synoptists supply us with many helpful details regarding these momentous hours, and the three accounts should be carefully compared. John, however, makes only brief reference to the supper and then proceeds to tell of the foot-washing—which was discussed earlier in this lesson. The brief passage from I Corinthians indicates how Jesus' instructions were later transmitted to the Christian converts, and also how Holy Communion formed an important part of the worship services in the Early Church.

When making a study of the happenings in the Upper Room and the institution of the Lord's Supper, it will be well to give special attention to several important details. Consider the following:

1. Secrecy: The synoptic writers indicate that while Jesus desired to keep the Passover with his disciples according to Jewish custom, he also took special precautions to keep secret the place where they were to partake of the supper. Why did Jesus make arrangements to observe the Passover in this way? What was the purpose of this secrecy? The answer seems to be of twofold nature: First, there was the desire to guard against intrusion. Jesus realized that this would be his final meeting with the disciples, and he had some very important instructions to convey to them. Hence, it would be

necessary to make this supper an exclusive "family affair" with no outsiders present. Second, Jesus also recognized that plans for his arrest had now taken definite shape, and his opponents would seize upon the first opportunity to carry him away. But Jesus' work was not yet complete, and he therefore guarded against the possibility of arrest at this time by keeping secret the location of the place where he planned to partake of the Passover supper.

2. Passover: The Passover was an annual feast, commemorating the deliverance of the Israelites from their Egyptian bondage, when the angel of death smote the first-born of the Egyptians but "passed over" the homes of the Israelites.[282] However, in studying the Christian Scriptures we must carefully distinguish between the Passover feast and the Lord's Supper. Jesus and his disciples sat down to partake of the Passover supper; but at the close of the meal Jesus instituted an entirely new observance, which we now speak of as the Lord's Supper. The Passover was a Jewish feast and is still observed annually by Jewish people; the Lord's Supper is the Christian sacrament which was instituted by Jesus "in the night in which he was betrayed." Thus, the Passover should be regarded as related to the teachings and activities of Moses; but the Lord's Supper comes to us direct from Jesus Christ and is observed by the Christian Church following his instructions.

---

[282] See Exodus 12

3. Nomenclature: The Lord's Supper is referred to under several different names in the various branches of the Christian church, and methods of observance also differ considerably. The terms most generally used should be familiar to you:
   1. The Lord's Supper.
   2. Holy Communion.
   3. The Sacrament.
   4. The Last Supper. This should not be applied to the Passover, but to the special observance instituted by Jesus following the Passover.
   5. Holy Eucharist or Festival of Joy.
   6. The Mass.
   7. The Agape or Love Feast. This term was used by the Early Church, and emphasized divine love as revealed through Jesus.
4. Judas: Sometimes the question is asked as to whether Judas was present when Jesus instituted the Lord's Supper. Matthew and Luke state that "the Twelve" sat down with Jesus to the Passover supper; this would include Judas. However, John mentions that Judas left the group before the Passover supper was completed, in order to give information regarding Jesus' possible location later in the evening. Nor could Judas have returned to the Upper Room, since he next appeared with the arresting officers in the garden of Gethsemane. Furthermore, the passage in I Corinthians (cited above) indicates that the Lord's Supper was instituted after the Passover observances had been

completed. Putting these details together, it would seem that Judas was not present when Jesus instituted this Christian sacrament, nor did Judas hear the Master say, "This do in remembrance of me."

5. Metaphysical Meaning: In seeking to understand the full significance of Holy Communion, it will be well at this point to make a careful reading of John 6:22-71. This passage tells how Jesus, earlier in his ministry, said to his hearers: "Except ye eat the flesh of the Son of man and drink his blood, ye have not life in yourselves ... for ... he that eats my flesh and drinks my blood abides in me, and I in him." But at that time neither Jesus' hearers nor his disciples could understand the meaning of these words, and we are told that "many walked no more with him." In the light of the happenings in the Upper Room, these words now take on new meaning; and through the symbology of Holy Communion, the followers of Jesus Christ are led into experiences of oneness with him. The following explanation of Holy Communion should prove helpful at this time: [283]

"The benefit of taking Holy Communion is the establishing of our acceptance of the Christ whose coming we celebrate within our mind and heart. The bread used in the churches symbolizes substance, which we consider the Lord's body, a body of spiritual ideas; and the wine used

---

[283] Fillmore, Charles *Keep a True Lent*, pp. 192-93

symbolizes his blood, which we consider life, or the circulation of divine ideas in our consciousness that will purify our mind and heart and renew our strength, freeing us from all corruption, sin, and evil, and bringing forth in us the abundant, unlimited life of God. Through the appropriation and assimilation of the substance and life in our own consciousness, we blend our mind with the Father-Mind and there is a harmonizing of every fiber of our body with the Christ body, which is life and light. As our mind and heart are cleansed of untrue thoughts and beliefs, and as we feed on living ideas, our body takes on the life and light of our divinity, and eventually will become living light".

The Closing Hymn: Matthew's Gospel tells how the activities in the Upper Room came to a close, and "when they had sung a hymn, they went out into the mount of Olives".[284] This "hymn" was known as the "Hallel", meaning "Praise", and consisted of Psalms 113-118—and the singing of this selection, or part thereof, was always included in the Passover celebration. In view of what was to follow, it is interesting to note some of the wording:

> *"Not unto us, O Jehovah, not unto us,*
> *But unto thy name give glory . . .*
> *I love Jehovah, because he hears*
> *My voice and my supplications....*
> *What shall I render unto Jehovah?*

---

[284] Matthew 26:30

For all his benefits toward me?
I will take the cup of salvation,
And call upon the name of Jehovah. . . .
Open to me the gates of righteousness:
I will enter into them."

Thus did Jesus and his disciples go forth, with a song upon their lips, marching onward toward Gethsemane, and to the Cross!

Chapter 11 - End - or New Beginning?

Historical Questions

1. In which Gospel do we find the "Upper Room teaching"? Give chapter references. Compare this "Upper Room teaching" with the Sermon on the Mount (Matt. 5, 6, 7), and then list some similarities and also some differences in these two accounts of Jesus' teaching.

2. When and where was Jesus arrested? Using your own words, tell briefly what happened in the garden of Gethsemane.

3. At the trial of Jesus, two serious charges were laid against him. What were these charges? Where were they made? Explain why the change was made when Jesus was brought before Pilate.

4. List the "seven last words" of Jesus, giving the Scripture references for each statement. Also give a brief explanation with each statement, indicating what circumstances gave rise to the words uttered by Jesus.

5. Why was the body of Jesus placed so hurriedly in the garden tomb? Give the names of two persons taking a prominent part in the burial of Jesus.

Metaphysical Questions

1. Use your own words and explain briefly the metaphysical significance of Gethsemane. If possible, give an illustration showing what this would mean in our own experience.

2. Briefly explain the term Comforter, as used in John's Gospel. (John 14:16) How does an understanding of this word help us today?

3. How would you explain the statement, "Thy will be done"? (Matt. 26:39) What misunderstanding is frequently made when considering these words?

4. Metaphysically, what does the Cross symbolize? Give three instances from the "seven last words," showing how certain negative beliefs or attitudes should be "crossed out."

5. What was Pilate's question regarding Jesus? (Matt. 27:22) Does a similar question sometimes arise in present-day experience? If so, how should we deal with it?

Lesson Text

Chapter ten dealt with several happenings connected with what is usually termed the closing phase of Jesus' ministry. This lesson will cover some further happenings taking place during this important period. But just here a question arises which should be given careful consideration: Should we continue to think of this phase of Jesus' ministry in terms of "closing," or should we now recognize it as a time of a new beginning? True, certain happenings during this period seem to indicate finality; but as we have already seen, Jesus' purpose in returning to Jerusalem was to undertake a mighty work in his own person, thereby opening to all people "a new and living way" into the kingdom. Therefore, in studying the following happenings connected with this phase of Jesus' ministry, it will be well to see them as representing both an "end," and also a "new beginning." This will become clearer as we proceed with our study.

The Upper Room Teaching
Read the passage: John 14,15,16,17

After reading the passages given above, we should make a brief comparison between these and the Sermon on the Mount.[285] Several striking similarities will be noted, and also some marked differences. Both the Sermon on the Mount and the Upper Room teaching may be regarded as compact accounts of Jesus' discourses; both will be recognized as being highly important, to the original hearers and to us today. The Sermon in Matthew's Gospel is reported as being delivered on a "mountain," while the teaching in John's Gospel was given in an "upper room"— and mountain and upper room both represent, metaphysically, a high place (or state) of consciousness.

However, by way of contrast, it will be noticed that the Sermon on the Mount is presented in simple, objective language, while the Upper Room teaching appears in more' advanced, or metaphysical, form. Furthermore, the Sermon on the Mount seems to have been given during the early part of Jesus' ministry; but the Upper Room teaching finds its rightful place in the closing phase of the ministry.

What we should recognize here is that this Upper Room teaching is in fact a veritable gold mine for us. Almost every verse in these chapters has its own special message, and careful reading will be productive of rich

---

[285] Matthew 5,6,7

rewards. The following suggestions will indicate helpful possibilities along these lines.

Chapter 14

Verse 1. "Let not your heart be troubled." Emphasis should be placed on the word heart. Jesus did not promise freedom from trouble, for he said, "In the world ye have tribulation".[286] But Jesus also taught that if we hold steady at the center of our consciousness (the heart), nothing in the outer world can disturb us. In this verse also Jesus spells out the secret of the untroubled heart, when he says, "[You already] believe in God; [now] believe also in me."

Verse 2. Instead of "many mansions," read "many chambers" (or rooms). Earlier, the disciples asked, "Are they few that are saved?"[287] In this passage Jesus assures his followers that there will be ample accommodation in the kingdom (or the Father's house) for all who earnestly seek to enter therein.

Verses 5-10. Read very carefully the questions asked by Thomas and Philip, and note the answers given by Jesus.

Verse 27. Note the use of the words peace, and my peace. In the Bible many times the word peace was used as a regular form of greeting—and as such, lost much of its meaning. Hence, Jesus here points out that his peace is not "as the world giveth." The peace of Jesus Christ is indeed that "peace ... which passes all understanding".[288]

---

[286] John 16:33
[287] Luke 13:23
[288] Philippians 4:7

Read through this fourteenth chapter again, verse by verse, and note how many helpful and inspiring ideas, similar to the above, will arise. The same procedure should be followed with the succeeding chapters. Suggestions given below will open other possibilities.

Chapter 15

Verses 1-8. Note that the word vine here refers to the main stem, and not to the vine as a whole. This is important.

Verse 11. Jesus here uses the words joy—my joy, and says, "Your joy ... made full." With this understanding, should we continue to think of Jesus as "the Man of Sorrows"?

Verse 12. Note that the "new commandment" includes more than to "Love one another." Jesus' words are, "Love one another, even as I have loved you."

Verse 13. Here Jesus indicates that he is about to lay down his life—and it should be recalled that this was included in Jesus' purpose in returning to Jerusalem. However, the verse points to the highest expression of love until that time—for a man to lay down his life for his friends. But Jesus was then preparing to go a step beyond this and lay down his life for those who proclaimed themselves as his enemies!

Chapter 16

In this chapter, and also in several other places in this section, reference is made to the "Comforter." Nowadays, the word comforter is usually understood as meaning someone who soothes, consoles, or brings solace to a person in distress. But in the Bible the Greek word used is Paraclete, which means an advocate, or helper— literally, someone who stands by one, as a lawyer stands beside his client in court. We should also note that, basically, the word comfort means "with strength." Thus, the promise here given is that the Comforter or Holy Spirit shall come to us, to give us strength, courage, and all needed help in any disturbing or distressing situation that may arise.

Chapter 17

Here we stand on holy ground, for we are reading the prayer that Jesus prayed just prior to his experiences in Gethsemane and on the Cross. Frequently we make use of what is termed "the Lord's Prayer"; but it should be remembered that this is actually a prayer given by Jesus to his disciples, for their use. However, the prayer given in this seventeenth chapter of John is the intercessory prayer actually used by Jesus himself during the closing moments of his ministry. It will be well to note how the prayer opens: "Father, glorify thy Son, that the Son may glorify thee." Then Jesus follows with a prayer for his disciples, and all who should come after them: "I pray for them ... that they all may be one, even as we are ... Father, I desire that they also ... be with me where I am ... that the love wherewith thou loves me may be in them, and I in them."

Gethsemane

Read the passages: Matthew 26:30-56; Mark 14:26-52;
Luke 22:39-53; John 18:1-11

The scriptural passages given above tell of Jesus'
final visit to the garden of Gethsemane. Careful thought
should be given to the following details.

1. Gethsemane: This was a small orchard-garden,
   located at the foot of the Mount of Olives.
   Tradition states that this garden was the property
   of Mary Magdalene, and that it was with her
   permission that Jesus used this quiet place for
   evening talks with his disciples. The word
   Gethsemane means "olive press," indicating that
   this much-prized oil was extracted there.

2. Metaphysical meaning: Gethsemane indicates "the
   struggle that takes place within the consciousness
   when Truth is realized as the one reality. All the
   good is pressed out and saved and the error is
   denied away. This is often agony—the suffering
   that the soul undergoes in giving up its cherished
   idols or in letting go of human consciousness. The
   great work of everyone is to incorporate the Christ
   Mind in soul and body. The process of eliminating
   the old consciousness and entering into the new
   may be compared to Gethsemane, whose meaning
   is 'oil press,' 'press for extracting unguents, and
   ointments'; a press is an emblem of trial, distress,

agony, while oil points to Spirit and illumination".[289]

3. It will be noticed that on this occasion Jesus stationed some of the disciples at the gateway of the garden—apparently to guard against a surprise attack. Jesus also intimated that instead of the usual private talk with the disciples, this would be a period wherein to "watch and pray." All this would indicate that Jesus was fully aware of Judas' plot, and also that he desired some further time for preparation. However, the gospel writers state that these disciple-sentinels fell asleep, and thus failed to convey to Jesus the desired word of warning.

4. Jesus' prayers: Many find it difficult to reconcile the two important prayers uttered by Jesus at this time. John's Gospel records that just before leaving the Upper Room Jesus prayed, "Father, the hour is come: glorify thy Son"[290] —and the inference is that Jesus visualized himself as going forward into a triumphant experience. However, the Synoptic Gospels state that immediately upon entering the garden Jesus prayed again, saying, "Father ... remove this cup from me".[291] Luke adds that Jesus was "in agony as he prayed," with "great drops of blood falling from his forehead".[292] Thus, it would appear that Jesus was hesitating from partaking of "the cup," and shrinking from the difficult

---

[289] *Metaphysical Bible Dictionary*, p. 231
[290] John 17:1
[291] Mark 14:36
[292] Luke 22:44

experiences before him. Why should there be this great difference in the two prayers?

1. This apparent reversal of attitude may never be fully explained, since the Christian writers make no further mention of these prayers of Jesus. However, a suggestion has been made which may throw some light on the subject. It will be noticed that in the first prayer[293] Jesus prayed not only for himself, but also for his disciples. Jesus said, "I am no more in the world, and these are in the world".[294] This would indicate that while Jesus had attained a high state of consciousness wherein he realized that the world could not harm him, he also realized that his disciples were still vulnerable, and that they might be affected and harmed. At this time Jesus said to Peter, "I made supplication for thee, that thy faith fail not".[295] Even in the garden Jesus said to the disciples, "Watch and pray, that ye enter not into temptation".[296] It seems possible that the "bitter cup" of which Jesus spoke in his agonizing prayer referred not to his own suffering on the Cross, but to the impending failure of the disciples. Judas was already involved in the betrayal plot—with its terrible consequences. Peter also was fast heading toward his tragic denial and subsequent breakdown. Could it be, then, that Jesus' prayer in Gethsemane was what might be

---

[293] In John's Gospel
[294] John 17:11
[295] Luke 22:32
[296] Mark 14:38

termed a "last-ditch effort" to save the disciples? For himself, Jesus could face the Cross without fear; but he did not want his disciples to fail!

5. "Thy will be done": During Jesus' prayer in Gethsemane, he used the words, "Nevertheless, not my will, but thine, be done".[297] Since this statement is often misunderstood, the following quotation should prove helpful:[298]

    "Most of us have an innate shrinking from saying, 'Thy will be done.' Because of false teaching, and from associations, we have believed that this prayer, if answered, would take away from us all that gives us joy or happiness. Surely nothing could be further from the truth. Oh, how we have tried to crowd the broad love of God into the narrow limits of man's mind! The grandest, most generous, loving father that ever lived is but the least bit of God's fatherhood manifested through the flesh. God's will for us means more love, more purity, more power, more joy in our lives every day.

6. The arrest: Apparently the arresting officers anticipated some difficulty in recognizing Jesus in the semi-dark garden, so Judas decided to help them. He said, "Whomsoever I shall kiss, that is he: take him".[299] It should be noted that the kiss here referred to was not a mark of affection, but was a

---

[297] Luke 22:42
[298] Cady, H. Emilie *How I Used Truth*, pp. 31-32
[299] Matthew 26:48

regular form of greeting in those days. But it is important to observe Jesus' response to this greeting. Instead of reproaching Judas for his traitorous act (for Judas' scheme was known to Jesus), Jesus actually called him "friend"! This seems like an outstanding example of "turning the other cheek." It is also important to note how Jesus healed one of his attackers, who was wounded in making this arrest.

The Trial of Jesus

Read the passages: Matthew 26:57; Matthew 27:26; Mark 14:53; Mark 15:20; Luke 22:54; Luke 23:25; John 18:12; John 19:16

The passages listed above tell how, following his arrest in Gethsemane, Jesus was brought before the Jewish leaders, and serious charges were laid against him. Careful study of the gospel records discloses that Jesus was tried five times, before being finally condemned. These trials took place as follows:

1. Before Annas, the deposed high priest: Scripture states that Caiaphas was the ruling high priest at the time of Jesus' trial; but Annas, as high priest emeritus, still had considerable political influence. This first trial is recorded only in John's Gospel— possibly because John was present on this occasion. Mention is made of the fact that John had some family or personal connection with the high priest, and was therefore given permission to enter the house during this preliminary trial.

2. Before Caiaphas and the Sanhedrin (the supreme council and highest judicial tribunal of the Jewish nation): Annas, following the first hearing mentioned above, sent Jesus to Caiaphas, the ruling high priest. This second trial consisted of two hearings.

First, Caiaphas and a few selected leaders held a preliminary meeting with Jesus and sought to elicit from him a confession of words and actions contrary to Jewish law. The charges brought against Jesus included plotting to destroy the Temple, claiming to be the Son of God, and other forms of blasphemy; and the high priest's purpose was to establish these charges, so that Jesus might be condemned to death. The Gospels indicate that during this period Peter waited in the courtyard of the high priest's palace; and when challenged regarding his connection with Jesus, Peter vehemently denied all knowledge of his Lord.

Second, with the coming of daylight, the Sanhedrin was called into official session in accordance with the regulations governing that court. The assembled Sanhedrin then confirmed the findings of the preliminary court of inquiry as mentioned above, declaring that Jesus was guilty of blasphemy and should be condemned to death. However, this decision should be fully understood. At an earlier period Caiaphas had met with his fellow leaders, and they reached the decision that Jesus must be put to death.[300] Thus, this second

---

[300] See John 11:47-53

trial is revealed as a mere face-saving effort, since those so-called judges had already condemned Jesus and decided upon his death, even before his arrest. However, there was one weak feature in this condemnation: Capital punishment was the prerogative of the Roman courts, and the Romans would not allow the Jews to carry out an execution. Hence, a further trial was necessary.

3. Before Pontius Pilate, at the Praetorium: At this point a further difficulty arose. Before the Jewish court Jesus had been condemned for blasphemy, which was regarded as the blackest of crimes; but the Romans did not consider blasphemy as a crime punishable by death. Therefore, before the Roman court the charge had to be changed to insurrection against the Roman government. Jesus' accusers said that he had proclaimed himself to be a king. The Roman governor, Pilate, quickly saw through this subterfuge, and transferred the case to the court of the Jewish king, Herod.

4. Before King Herod: Apparently Herod took this move to be a compliment to himself—for previously there had been friction between Pilate and Herod, and Herod therefore accepted this maneuver as a "peace offering." Luke records that "Herod and Pilate became friends with each other that very day".[301] Thus was Jesus a veritable peacemaker, even when his enemies were seeking to destroy him!

---

[301] Luke 23:12

5. The final trial before Pontius Pilate: Here should be noted Pilate's repeated efforts to sidetrack the demands of the Jewish leaders. But all these efforts were of no avail, and Pilate finally pronounced the death sentence upon Jesus. And in this connection it should be noted that an inscription was placed on the Cross, over the head of Jesus: "THIS IS JESUS THE KING OF THE JEWS".[302] This would indicate that Jesus was executed because of the charge of insurrection, rather than because of the original charge of blasphemy.

Pilate's Question

Read the passages: Matthew 27:22; Mark 15:12-14; Luke 23:20-23; John 19:4-11

The above passages are quite brief, and may be read in a few minutes. Nevertheless, these passages should be given careful thought, for they contain a very important question. Pilate asked, "What then shall I do unto Jesus, who is called Christ?" And a somewhat similar question often arises in connection with our present-day experiences.

Metaphysically interpreted, Pilate represents "the ruling power of the sense plane, the carnal mind".[303] This "ruling power" also has a place in our consciousness, and is active in making decisions and ordering the final disposition of the problems and situations that confront us from time to time. Thus when a question arises—such as

---

[302] Matthew 27:37
[303] *Metaphysical Bible Dictionary*, p. 350

indicated in the above Bible passages—this "ruling power" is called upon to make a decision; and the following possibilities should be considered.

1. Like Pilate, we may seek to evade the issue, or pass it along for others to make the decision. However, this is only a temporary expedient, for the question is one to which we must give a definite answer.

2. Like Pilate, we may make the wrong decision and thus eliminate the highest good from our life and affairs. We should here recall how Pilate yielded to the clamor of the crowd and sent Jesus to the Cross.

3. Unlike Pilate, we may make a right decision, recognizing the place of the Christ in our life and affairs, and calling upon him to take full control. Such a decision immediately brings about a startling reversal of the original question; for instead of continuing to ask, "What shall I do unto Jesus?" we find that he can do something truly wonderful to and for us. He can bring about a complete transformation in our life and affairs. Perhaps this is what Paul had in mind, when he wrote, "Wherefore, if any man is in Christ, he is a new creature".[304]

The Crucifixion

Read the passages: Matthew 27:27-56; Mark 15:16-41; Luke 23:26-49; John 19:1-37

---

[304] II Corinthians 5:17

All four Gospels tell of Jesus' crucifixion. The passages listed above record the historical facts, and these should be carefully studied. Some slight differences will be noted in the various accounts, but essentially the story is the same.

However, when reading these accounts of Jesus' crucifixion, certain poignant questions are likely to arise and the we should be prepared to deal with these. For example, we may ask: Why did Jesus go to the Cross? What purpose was served by the Crucifixion? How should we interpret those tragic events that brought Jesus' ministry to such a distressing close? The following suggestions should be given very careful consideration.

1. Martyrdom: Some historians have suggested that the Crucifixion should be regarded as a form of martyrdom. A martyr is usually regarded as one who is put to death because of his adherence to religious principles, or one who suffers as the result of promulgating certain teachings. With this definition in mind, Jesus could be regarded as a martyr—similar to Stephen, James, Peter, Paul, and many other Christian leaders. However, we usually think of Jesus as being something more than a martyr, and therefore the Crucifixion calls for further explanation.

2. Vicarious sacrifice: Theologically, since Christian times the Crucifixion has been regarded as a sacrifice for the sin of the world, and most are familiar with the term "vicarious sacrifice." The early Christians knew of the daily sacrifices at

the Temple in Jerusalem; but they came to regard these sacrifices as temporary, while the sacrifice on the Cross was final and complete. Thus, the writer of the Epistle to the Hebrews states: "Every priest indeed stands day by day ministering and offering sometimes the same sacrifices, the which can never take away sins; but he [Jesus], when he had offered one sacrifice for sins forever, sat down on the right hand of God: henceforth expecting till his enemies be made the footstool of his feet. For by one offering he hath perfected forever them that are sanctified".[305] The Apostle Paul writes about "Jesus ... who was delivered up for our transgressions".[306] Jesus also stated that "The Son of man came ... to give his life a ransom for many";[307] and when instituting the Lord's Supper, he said, "This is my blood of the covenant, which is poured out for many unto remission of sins".[308] The Christian Scriptures contain many similar passages; and, as already indicated, this teaching has been generally accepted by Christian theologians.

3. Overcoming: There is one aspect of the Crucifixion which seems to have been largely overlooked in the development of Christian teaching; but if we are to fully understand the

---

[305] Hebrews 10:11-14
[306] Romans 4:24-25
[307] Matthew 20:28
[308] Matthew 26:28

meaning of the Cross, this should now be given careful consideration. In the opening section of this lesson the statement was made that "Jesus' purpose in returning to Jerusalem was to undertake a mighty work in his own person." The Gospel accounts show how Jesus, in the outworking of this purpose, advanced step by step toward the Cross. But a careful study of all the factors involved shows clearly that Jesus' purpose in going to the Cross included something greater than martyrdom or sacrifices—although these may appear to be very important. The Bible makes clear that Jesus, by his work on the Cross, met and overcame "the last dread enemy of mankind"—death—and thereby opened for all people "a new and living way" into the kingdom, and into the experience of eternal life. Earlier in his ministry Jesus said, "My sheep ... follow me: and I give unto them eternal life".[309] Such a gift became possible because of Jesus' mighty victory over death on the Cross. All this was fully recognized by the apostles and the early Church, as is shown by statement after statement in the Christian Scriptures: "Our Savior Christ Jesus, who abolished death, and brought life and immortality to light";[310] "As sin reigned in death, even so might grace reign through righteousness unto eternal life through

---

[309] John 10:27-28
[310] II Timothy 1:10

Jesus Christ our Lord";[311] "For as in Adam all die, so also in Christ shall all be made alive";[312] "Death is swallowed up in victory ... thanks be to God, who giveth us the victory through our Lord Jesus Christ".[313]

The Seven Last Words

Read the passages: Luke 23:33-38; Luke 23:39-43; John 19:25-27; John 19:28-29; Matthew 27:45-50; Mark 15:33-37; Psalms 22; John 19:30; Luke 23:44-46; Genesis 2:1-3.

The "last words" or statements uttered by Jesus while he was on the Cross are included in the scriptural passages given at the head of this lesson. However, it will be noticed that none of the Gospels contains all the statements. The complete list of seven statements, as generally recognized, is arrived at by combining the information given in all four Gospels.

Metaphysically, the Cross symbolizes a process of "crossing out" certain error beliefs that have been given a place in our consciousness. Nor is this a mere play on words. At the time of Jesus, the Romans used the punishment of the cross as a means of eradicating or crossing out wrongdoing from the land. It will be recalled that two thieves or highway robbers were crucified alongside Jesus—while Jesus was crucified for the alleged crime of insurrection. Similarly, in a metaphysical way, we seek to "cross out" those erroneous beliefs and conditions

---

[311] Romans 5:21
[312] I Corinthians 15:22
[313] I Corinthians 15:43-57

which tend to mar and spoil our life and affairs. The preceding section of this lesson indicated how Jesus sought to "cross out" those dominating beliefs of sin and death through his Crucifixion; but in uttering his last words Jesus also indicated that there were some other error beliefs that needed to be "crossed out." Thus, even from the Cross, Jesus was giving some very important teaching. The significance of all this is seen when we recall how Jesus had said earlier, "If any man would come after me, let him ... take up his cross, and follow me".[314] These seven last words of Jesus should therefore be given careful consideration.

First Word: "Father, forgive them, for they know not what they do."[315]

This statement had reference to all persons who opposed Jesus during his ministry, as well as to those who actually sent him to the cross and crucified him. Metaphysically, this would indicate that all negative beliefs of resentment, bitterness, hatred, ill will and the like are to be "crossed out" by an act of forgiveness. Sometimes there is a tendency for us to rationalize, claiming that we have legitimate reasons, or "the right," to hold such thoughts. But such an attitude still leaves us in the bondage of error thought. Freedom is found only through forgiveness.

---

[314] Matthew 16:24
[315] Luke 23:33-38

Second Word: "Today shalt thou be with me in Paradise."[316]

The general tendency is to interpret this statement as a promise regarding entry into some favored state, or place, in the hereafter. When these words were uttered, both Jesus and the penitent thief were suffering on their crosses; but it is implied that when this suffering was ended the thief would join Jesus in "Paradise." However, looking carefully into the context, we find the penitent thief making this request: "Jesus, remember me when you come into thy kingdom." Thus, the thief was projecting the kingdom into the future—"when thou come." But this was contrary to Jesus' teaching, for he stated that the kingdom is here, now.[317] This might be difficult to understand—especially under such circumstances! Nevertheless, Jesus made it clear that the experience of the kingdom does not depend upon time or circumstances, but may be attained even within the framework of the Cross. It is most important to recognize how Jesus changed the emphasis from "when" to "today." In other words, we must "cross out" the belief that our good is to be projected into, or is dependent upon, the future; and we must claim our good in the here and now. This attitude is expressed in the well-known hymn:

> *"Nearer, my God, to Thee, Nearer to Thee!*
> *E'en though it be a cross that raises me."*

---

[316] Luke 23:39-43
[317] See Luke 17:20-21

Third Word: "Woman, behold, thy son! ... Behold, thy mother!"[318]

This is a well-known passage, and it reveals something of Jesus' way of thinking. Somehow, he always managed to think of others first. Even on the Cross, his thought was for others. First he prayed for his persecutors; then he gave a word of encouragement to the penitent thief; and finally, there was this thoughtful provision for the sorrowing mother, Mary. The presence of John at this time should also be noted. All the other disciples had fled in terror when Jesus was arrested; but John followed Jesus, even to the Cross.

Metaphysically, both Mary and John symbolize love, and Jesus' action at this time brings out a very important teaching concerning love. Scripture instructs us to "love God," and to "love one another" —and these instructions are always regarded as paramount. But if love is to amount to anything worthwhile, it must be put into action. Love has been defined as the law of giving and receiving carried to the highest point of expression. Thus, the teaching here is that we must "cross out" the notion that thinking and talking about love is sufficient; we must actually do something about love—just as Jesus did. Love is best expressed, not by words, but by deeds. Shortly before the crucifixion, Jesus said, "If ye love me, ye will keep my commandments".[319]

---

[318] John 19:25-27
[319] John 14:15

Fourth Word: "I thirst."[320]

This is a very brief statement, and seems to refer to an urgent physical need. The circumstances would indicate that Jesus must have suffered from thirst at that time. However, there is a thirst beyond the physical; and several times during his ministry Jesus used the word in a spiritual sense. He said, "Blessed are they that hunger and thirst after righteousness".[321] Also, when speaking to the Samaritan woman at the well, Jesus said, "Every one that drinks of this water shall thirst again: but whosoever drinks of the water that I shall give him shall never thirst".[322] Perhaps, therefore, we should interpret this statement from the Cross as instruction to "cross out" the erroneous thought that material things can satisfy our longings and "thirsts." Man is a spiritual being; and only that which is spiritual can fully satisfy his thirst.

Fifth Word: "My God, my God, why hast thou forsaken me?"[323]

This is usually regarded as the most difficult of the words from the Cross. At first reading, it seems to indicate that Jesus had abandoned all hope, feeling that God had utterly failed him. No wonder this passage is regarded as difficult! Scripture states that some of the bystanders at the Cross completely misunderstood the import of Jesus' words; so there may be some excuse for similar misunderstandings by present-day readers.

---

[320] John 19:28,29
[321] Matthew 5:6
[322] John 4:13-14
[323] Matthew 27:45-50; Mark 15:33-37; Psalm 22

However, the situation is somewhat clarified when we realize that Jesus was quoting from the opening verse of the Twenty-second Psalm. We should therefore refer to this psalm, and read it carefully from beginning to end. It will be noticed that the 22 Psalm consists of two main sections. The first section[324] expresses the anguish of the human heart during periods of severe trial. At such a time it may seem that God has withdrawn his presence and power. But the second section of the psalm[325] shows the response of what we sometimes term "the indwelling Spirit." In other words, there is the realization that despite all appearances God is still with us, and at the right moment his salvation will be made manifest. Notice how the Psalmist expresses his trust in God:

"Ye that fear Jehovah, praise him . . .

For he hath not despised nor abhorred the affliction of the afflicted; neither hath he hid his face from him; but when he cried, he heard."[326]

Metaphysically, this indicates that we should "cross out" all erroneous thoughts about God withdrawing his protecting presence from us—no matter what appearances may indicate. We should realize that "in him we live, and move, and have our being"[327]—and that in all our experiences, nothing "shall be able to separate us from the love of God, which is in Christ Jesus our Lord".[328]

---

[324] Verses 1-21
[325] Verses 22-31
[326] Psalms 22:23-24
[327] Acts 17:28
[328] Romans 8:39

Sixth Word: "It is finished."[329]

There are two possible interpretations of this statement. We may regard the words as indicating that Jesus' ministry had come to a tragic end. He had tried his best; but apparently all his efforts had failed, and all the bright hopes regarding the kingdom had sunk into oblivion. However, in the light of subsequent events, we are now able to see that the words "It is finished" actually represent a cry of triumph. Jesus' ministry had not failed—notwithstanding all the efforts of those who opposed him. A few hours before the crucifixion, Jesus said, "Be of good cheer; I have overcome the world".[330] And now, even "the last dread enemy, death" was overcome, and the "new and living way" was opened into the kingdom.

This would indicate that we should "cross out" all thoughts relating to the inadequacy or failure of Jesus' ministry. At an earlier period a wavering John the Baptizer inquired, "Art thou he that cometh, or look we for another?"[331] John was not privileged to see Jesus' ministry carried to its completion, whereas we now have the complete story. Therefore, we should "cross out" all negative or limiting beliefs. The Bible states emphatically that Jesus' ministry was fully complete, and that his was the final word. "God, having of old time spoken unto the fathers in the prophets ... hath at the end of these days spoken unto us in his Son".[332] And the Apostles Peter and John fearlessly proclaimed: "In none other is there

---

[329] John 19:30
[330] John 16:33
[331] Matthew 11:3
[332] Hebrews 1:1

salvation: for neither is there any other name under heaven that is given among men, wherein we must be saved".[333]

Seventh Word: "Father, into thy hands I commend my spirit."[334]

Two important features should be noted here.

The significant change from "My God," to "Father." As was stated earlier, the Fifth Word from the Cross was a direct quotation from Scripture; but in the Seventh Word Jesus returned to the divine name which he used so frequently during his ministry. Thus, in making present-day application of these terms, the words My God may symbolize a knowledge of God; while the term Father would indicate an intimate and loving relationship.

The Seventh Word also indicates how we may "cross out" all fears or feelings of apprehension regarding the future, by placing all our affairs "lovingly in the hands of the Father." It is interesting and instructive to notice how, in the story of the Creation,[335] the six periods of creative activity were followed by the divinely-planned seventh period of rest. Similarly, all the "crossing out" activity, as indicated by the Words from the Cross, culminates in the realization of resting in the love of the Father. All activity connected with the Cross reaches a point where "it is finished"; but the Father's love continues forever.

---

[333] Acts 4:12
[334] Luke 23:44-46 and Genesis 2:1-3
[335] As given in Genesis 1:1-2:3

The Garden Tomb

Read the passages: Matthew 27:57-66; Mark 15:42-47;
Luke 23:50-56; John 19:38-42

The above passages give a clear account of the
events immediately following the crucifixion and the
entombment of the body of Jesus. However, some brief
notes regarding two persons mentioned will be in order.

It will be noticed that Nicodemus is mentioned only
in John's Gospel. During the early period of Jesus' ministry,
Nicodemus came to Jesus "by night".[336] Later, Nicodemus
incurred the displeasure of the Jewish leaders by an
attempted defense of Jesus.[337] Nicodemus also took part
in the entombment activities, as recorded in the passage
given above. Questions are sometimes raised regarding
Nicodemus' attitude during the trial of Jesus. Why did he
not raise his voice in protest? Several possibilities have
been suggested; but the most likely reason seems to be
that Nicodemus, still somewhat skeptical, felt that if Jesus
was really the Messiah, he would surely declare himself,
and thus overcome his enemies.

Joseph of Arimathea is mentioned as being a
disciple "in secret"—yet he seems to have displayed great
courage in claiming the body of Jesus and having it
carefully placed in his own prepared tomb. However, at
that time, the burial of strangers was regarded as a work
of great piety, and acts of that sort would have been
regarded with approbation by the Jewish leaders. The
Book of Tobit, in the Hebrew Apocrypha, tells how its hero

---

[336] John 3:1-21
[337] John 7:45-52

buried several Jews who had been murdered by oppressors; and Joseph of Arimathea would have been quite familiar with this story. Tradition states that, following the resurrection of Jesus, Joseph became an ardent Christian, and legend has it that he was instrumental in carrying the Gospel to Britain.

Chapter 12 - He Lives!

Historical Questions

1. Did the disciples regard the Crucifixion as the end of Jesus' ministry—or did they expect a resurrection? Give reasons for your answer, with Bible references.

2. Use your own words and tell briefly the story of Easter morning. (Follow the sequence of events as recorded in John 20:1-18.)

3. After telling the Easter story, what substantiating evidence (or "proofs") of Jesus' resurrection could you put forward? List several important points, with a brief explanation of each.

4. Mention, and explain briefly, two important tasks that confronted Jesus during the forty-day period between his resurrection and ascension. Make clear what Jesus was seeking to impart to the disciples at that time.

5. List the Bible passages which tell of Jesus' ascension, stating briefly what these passages indicate. Also mention the important assurance given in Matthew's Gospel.

Metaphysical Questions

1. Explain briefly the place and purpose of resurrection in our experience. What is indicated by the term "daily resurrections"?

2. What is the purpose of spiritual baptism? Explain briefly the difference between this and water baptism. When, and how, is spiritual baptism received?

3. Explain briefly the difference between intellectual understanding and spiritual understanding. How was this difference shown in the words and actions of Thomas? (See John 20:24-29.)

4. Mention some important present-day lessons arising from the Emmaus story. (See Luke 24:13-35.) What does Cleopas symbolize?

5. What does the ascension of Jesus Christ represent in our consciousness? How is ascension related to resurrection? How is ascension to be attained?

Lesson Text

At the dawn of each Easter Day, Christians everywhere join in singing joyous hymns which proclaim the resurrection of Jesus Christ. Easter is always a season of rejoicing! The darkness and gloom of Good Friday give place to the brightness and joy of the Resurrection Day. We, no matter what season may be indicated on the calendar, also may enter into joyous Easter experiences when, after contemplating the Cross, we turn to the story of the Resurrection.

"Christ the Lord is risen today, Alleluia!
Sons of men and angels say: Alleluia!
Raise your joys and triumphs high, Alleluia!
Sing, ye heavens, and earth reply, Alleluia!"

However, before entering upon a detailed study of the various happenings which will be discussed in this lesson, it will be well to recognize the close relationship between the Cross and the Resurrection. These should not be thought of as separate events, but rather as integral parts of one great whole. The Cross may be regarded as symbolizing the negative, or denial, phase of the story; while the positive, or affirmative, phase is shown in the Resurrection. The Cross marks the overcoming of all those beliefs and influences which tend to mar and spoil life—such as bondage, evil, sin, and death; while the Resurrection demonstrates victory over all these, and reveals the perfect pattern of the life abundant and eternal. This relationship should be kept well in mind when studying the following phases of the Easter story:

Easter Morning
Read the passage: John 20:1-18; Matt. 28:1-10; Mark 16:1-11; Luke 24:1-12

The resurrection story is told in all four Gospels. Each account should be carefully read, and the details compared. John's Gospel gives the clearest picture of the momentous happenings at the garden tomb on Easter morning, and special consideration should be given to the following significant features:

Mary's purpose in visiting the tomb: John's Gospel makes it clear that Mary did not go forth on Easter morning to greet the risen Lord. Her purpose was to perform those last loving rites connected with the entombment, which had not been completed following the Crucifixion. It will be recalled that the body of Jesus had been hurriedly taken from the Cross and deposited in the tomb because of the approaching Sabbath Day; for nothing could be done after six o'clock on Friday evening.[338] But just as soon as the Sabbath had passed, Mary Magdalene came to the tomb "on the first day of the week ... early, while it was yet dark." This is an indication of Mary's desire to complete the necessary arrangements at the earliest possible moment. However, she was unable to carry out her cherished plans, for she was distressed to find that the body of Jesus was no longer in the tomb. The stone had been removed from the entrance, and the hurriedly-deposited body had vanished.

The activities of Peter and John: The Gospel tells how Mary hurried to the house where the two disciples had taken refuge, and in a distracted way told them of her startling discovery. Peter and John thereupon hurried to the tomb—with John, the younger man, outrunning Peter. At the entrance of the tomb John came to a sudden halt, apparently becoming fearful of ceremonial contamination, and he waited the arrival of Peter. But Peter seems to have had no similar qualms, for he went into the tomb, and was followed by John. The Gospel states that the two disciples "saw and believed"[339] —but the context indicates that this has no reference to belief in the Resurrection. The two disciples saw that the tomb was empty, and they believed what Mary had told them, Vis: that someone had removed the body of Jesus. The importance of this will be discussed later.

Mary and the "Gardener": Again, it should be noted that at that time Mary's great concern was regarding the disappearance of the body of her beloved Master. Her question to the "Gardener" indicated how

---

[338] See Luke 23:54 and John 19:40-42
[339] John 20:8

great her desire to complete the burial rites was. Only when the "Gardener" replied, speaking her name in those well-remembered tones—"Mary!" —did she enter upon her first realization of the Resurrection.

Easter Evening
Read the passages: Mark 16:12-13; Luke 24:13-35

The Journey to Emmaus: The brief reference in Mark's Gospel, telling of the two disciples meeting the risen Lord "as they walked, on their way into the country," is expanded into a very interesting and detailed story in Luke's Gospel. Very little is known about these two travelers, since one is unnamed, while the other is briefly referred to as "Cleopas." Certainly, they were not members of the innermost group ("the Twelve"), but there are some indications that Cleopas was related to the family of Jesus; hence he would have been familiar with the recent happenings at Jerusalem and the tragedy of the Cross. Some additional light is thrown on the story through the metaphysical interpretation of the name Cleopas.

"A faculty of mind not yet awakened fully to spiritual understanding. It has heard the Truth: Cleopas was a follower of Jesus; he had walked and talked with him, but he had never affirmed as his own the Truth that Jesus taught. Through the blessing and breaking of bread his eyes were opened— his comprehension was cleared— and he realized the Truth as his own".[340]

We may be inclined to ask why the two travelers did not recognize Jesus. It must be recalled that this was

---

[340] *Metaphysical Bible Dictionary*, p. 153

not merely a casual meeting. Jesus was with them for several hours, and he talked freely with them. Why, then, was there this lack of recognition? The Gospel writer seems to have anticipated this question, for he explains that "their eyes were opened that they should not know him".[341] But two other things should be taken into consideration:

1. Possible difference in Jesus' clothing. It will be recalled that Jesus' garments had been stripped from him at the time of the Crucifixion, so he might now be appearing in unfamiliar clothing; and this might have prevented ready recognition.
2. The two men knew that Jesus had been crucified, and had been taken from the Cross, and buried. Therefore, under such circumstances, the thought of meeting him on the Emmaus road would be furthest from their minds.

The intriguing feature of this story is found in the closing statement, which reads, "He was known of them in the breaking of bread".[342] This could scarcely have reference to the previous breaking of bread in the upper room on the night before the Crucifixion—since at that time the story of the Lord's Supper would not have been communicated to the two travelers. It seems much more likely that Jesus used the same form of table blessing at Emmaus that he had used many times before during his ministry,[343] and that it was because of this repetition that Jesus became known to them. There is also the further

---

[341] Luke 24:16
[342] Luke 24:35
[343] See Matthew 14:19 and Mark 8:6

possibility that in giving the blessing at Emmaus, Jesus raised his hands, disclosing the nail prints still visible there, and thus revealing his identity. The two travelers asked, "Was not our heart burning within us, while he spoke to us in the way?" Perhaps on the journey they had partly recognized the familiar voice; but when they sat at table and saw the nail prints in his hands, they knew then that they were in the presence of the risen Lord.

In the Upper Room
Read the passages: John 20:19-29

Several important points should be noted here: Jesus' appearance in the upper room: Apparently, Mary Magdalene's story regarding the risen Lord had been communicated to the disciples, and they had hurriedly gathered in the upper room, hoping to receive some confirmation of the startling news. This confirmation came with the personal appearance of Jesus himself—and the Gospel writer states that the disciples "were glad when they saw the Lord." John also mentions that the doors of the room were shut and, presumably, securely fastened. Nevertheless, Jesus entered the room and stood there with his disciples. However, Luke reports that at approximately the same time Jesus was talking with the two travelers at Emmaus—as discussed earlier in this lesson. These two happenings would therefore seem to indicate that the risen Lord had entered upon a new dimensional experience, since he was then transcending the limitations of space and time.

The spiritual baptism: Scripture states that when Jesus met his disciples in the upper room, "he breathed on them, and said ... Receive ye the Holy Spirit".[344] This happening should be associated with a statement of John the Baptizer, when he said: "I indeed baptize you in water ... but he ... shall baptize you in the Holy Spirit".[345] It is significant that Jesus, during his early ministry, did not concern himself overmuch with the outer ceremony of baptism.[346] But at the time now being discussed, Jesus is seen administering spiritual baptism to his disciples. Some are puzzled regarding the statement, "he breathed on them." This should be compared with Genesis 2:7, which reads: "And Jehovah God formed man ... and breathed into his nostrils the breath of life; and man became a living soul." The Genesis account tells of the first, or physical, creation; but the breathing activity mentioned in John's Gospel symbolizes the new, or spiritual, creation.

The second upper-room meeting: The scriptural account states that "after eight days" the disciples again met in the upper room, and Jesus also appeared to them at that time. It should be noted that, according to the Jewish custom of numbering, both "first days" would be included in this reckoning. Thus, the first upper-room meeting was held on Easter evening (Sunday), while the second meeting was on the Sunday (or first day) of the following week. The question may be asked: Why did the disciples reassemble in the upper room on this second "first day"? There are several possibilities:

---

[344] John 20:22
[345] Matthew 3:11
[346] See John 4:2

1. When meeting with the disciples on Easter evening, Jesus may have instructed them to meet again on the following week;
2. The disciples may have been so impressed with the events of Easter that they decided to meet again on the following "first day";
3. It is significant that quite early in Christian history, the followers of Jesus met regularly on the first day of the week, and they referred to this as "the Lord's Day."[347]

Activities of Thomas

The term doubter is frequently applied to the Apostle Thomas, and this originated in Thomas' unwillingness to accept the testimony of his fellow apostles concerning the appearance of Jesus. Taking all circumstances into consideration, his attitude is understandable. After seeing the lifeless body of Jesus taken from the Cross and laid in the tomb, who could have believed the story of Jesus' appearance in the upper room? We should give very careful attention to Thomas' second statement— words uttered when Jesus appeared and spoke to him. At that time Thomas not only accepted the truth of the Resurrection, but he also cried, "My Lord, and my God!" Here, it should be noted, Thomas was openly proclaiming the divinity of Jesus Christ. Present-day readers of the Bible are familiar with Thomas' statement and therefore may not recognize its full significance. At the time of utterance, however, such a statement could have brought upon Thomas the charge of blasphemy —and this

---

[347] Acts 20:7; I Corinthians 16:2; Revelation 1:10

was punishable by death. Perhaps the time has now come when the name of Thomas should be removed from the "doubter" category, and placed where it really belongs— among the names of brave men! Some further noteworthy statements by Thomas are given in John 11:16 and John 14:5-7.

Metaphysical Significance

The historical background given above indicates why, in metaphysical interpretation, Thomas is used as a symbol for "understanding." There are two phases of understanding, and both are easily recognized in the words and actions of Thomas:

1. Intellectual understanding—arrived at by intellectual processes. It will be noted that Thomas desired to have "proofs" to substantiate belief,
2. Spiritual understanding— attained through illumination.

When Thomas finally attained this illumination, he had no need to "see" or "touch"—he knew! Jesus referred to these two phases of understanding when he said, "Because thou hast seen me, thou hast believed; blessed are they that have not seen, yet have believed".[348]

Proofs of Resurrection

Read the passages: Matthew 28:11-15; I Corinthians 15:12 - 19

All four Gospels present the story of Jesus' resurrection, and this important phase of his ministry is

---

[348] John 20:29

recognized by Christian people everywhere. Year after year the happenings of the first Easter morning are gladly recalled, and the resurrection of Jesus Christ is a firmly established fact in history. Nevertheless, we should be aware that in the early days there were some persons who challenged the story of the Resurrection. The Jewish leaders not only refused to recognize Jesus as Messiah, but they also sought to explain away his resurrection. Some activities in this connection are indicated in the Christian Scriptural passages given above. Therefore, it may be well for the us to consider carefully some substantiating facts connected with the Resurrection:

The testimony of the Apostles: The Gospels make clear that at first the Apostles, and other followers of Jesus, were prepared to accept the crucifixion and burial as final. True, during his ministry Jesus had mentioned the resurrection; but, apparently, all such teaching had been driven from the minds of his followers by the tragic happenings of Good Friday. Mary went to the tomb early on Easter morning to anoint the body of Jesus, not to greet the risen Lord. Peter and John believed that the body of Jesus had been taken from the tomb and buried elsewhere. Thomas refused to believe that there had been a resurrection. Yet all these, and many more, were eventually convinced. This was more than an out-picturing of "wishful thinking." This was an acceptance of a demonstration which they had heretofore deemed impossible. They were "convinced against their will," but they were not "of the same opinion still"! They who had not at first believed testified that Jesus was risen indeed.

The extra testimony: When reading the gospel accounts of the Resurrection, we are likely to suppose that all these stories originated with persons very close to Jesus. The tendency, therefore, may be to regard such testimony as somewhat biased. But the Apostle Paul states that shortly after the Resurrection the risen Lord was seen by "above five hundred brethren"—and this in addition to the persons closely associated with Jesus.[349] A dozen disciples might have been biased or mistaken; but the testimony of five hundred persons surely demands serious recognition.

The gospel records: It is important to recognize that the Synoptic Gospels were in circulation as early as 65-75 CE. This means that at that time there would have been many persons living who could remember the actual happenings connected with the Crucifixion and the Resurrection. Thus, had the gospel stories of the Resurrection been inaccurate, they would have been refuted and would soon have become nonexistent. Under such circumstances, the survival of the Resurrection stories must therefore be regarded as proof of their authenticity.

The changed attitude of the Apostles: Immediately following the arrest of Jesus, all his followers fled in terror and went into hiding. Peter actually declared vehemently that he had no connection with Jesus. But immediately following the Resurrection the Apostles reappeared and began to move about Jerusalem, not fearing what the authorities might do to them. Indeed, at quite an early period, Peter proclaimed the Resurrection in an area

---

[349] I Corinthians 15:6

adjacent to the spot where Jesus had been condemned to death. The Apostles were changed men. Nor were these changes brought about by any "cunningly devised fables." Such transformations can be accounted for only through the reality of the Resurrection.

Extension of the teaching: It should be further noted that, in addition to the Gospels, the Resurrection teaching has a prominent place in the Epistles of the Bible. This indicates that the Resurrection was fully recognized throughout the Early Church. Indeed, the Resurrection formed one of the basic teachings of the Early Church. Early Christians thought not of a dead hero, but of the risen Christ; apart from the Resurrection, there would have been no Christian church. Thus, the very existence of the Christian church constitutes a very important piece of evidence as to the reality of the Resurrection.

Interpretation of the Resurrection

When studying the life and activities of Jesus, many persons regard his resurrection as the high point in his ministry. Certainly, Jesus' victory over death and the grave must be recognized as an outstanding achievement. The stupendous happenings of the first Easter morning marked the beginning of a new era in history, and Christian people everywhere continue to commemorate and rejoice in the resurrection of Jesus. But when attempting to understand present-day teaching regarding the Resurrection, we may encounter two seemingly different lines of thought:

There are some persons who, while accepting the Resurrection as a historical fact, regard it as applying exclusively to Jesus. They believe that the Resurrection was the crowning point of Jesus' ministry; that it was a convincing demonstration of his divinity; and that the events of Easter morning proclaimed to the world that Jesus was indeed the Son of God. They are willing to recognize that the Resurrection has been an inspiration to all followers of Jesus, both in ancient and present times; but they also hold that the actual Resurrection had its beginning and ending in Jesus himself.

There are other persons who believe that Jesus' resurrection was a "first fruits of them that are asleep".[350] They see in Jesus' resurrection a representation of something which is to take place in our experience—"For as in Adam all die, so also in Christ shall all be made alive". Thus, Jesus was the Way-Shower; and just as he died and rose again, so also may we look toward a resurrection in our experience. Thus far the teaching is clear. But the question arises: When does our resurrection take place? We can date the resurrection of Jesus as being on the first Easter morning; but when shall we experience a like resurrection? Many Christian theologians point to a distant time, usually designated as "the last day," and assure us that that will be our day of resurrection. Indeed, this "last day" and the "day of resurrection" have become almost synonymous terms.

What should be our attitude—toward the Bible message? Several things seem fairly clear:

Jesus taught that we should share in his resurrection: "I am the resurrection, and the life; he that believeth on me, though he die, yet shall he live";[351]

---

350 I Corinthians 15:20
351 John 11:25

"Because I live, ye shall live also".[352] Jesus also said, "he that believeth on me, the works that I do shall he do also"[353] —and we must surely include resurrection among the "works" of Jesus!

It is also noticeable that in some early writings the resurrection of Christian believers is projected to a future time—the time of "the coming of the Lord."[354] This would indicate that this teaching was familiar to the Early Christians.

But in later Bible writings, resurrection is often referred to as a present experience— an experience which is to be entered upon here and now. Writing to the Ephesians, the Apostle Paul states: "And you he did make alive, when ye were dead through your trespasses and sins, wherein ye once walked ... but God ... even when we were dead through our trespasses, made us alive together with Christ ... and raised us up with him, and made us to sit with him in the heavenly places in Christ Jesus".[355] This is followed by an urgent call: "Awake, thou that sleep, and arise from the dead, and Christ shall shine upon thee".[356] The Apostle also wrote to the Colossians, "If then ye were raised with Christ, seek the things that are above".[357] There are also other similar passages. Thus it would appear that in the Early Church the word resurrection also indicated an experience to be sought after and attained by the Christians.

---

[352] John 14:19
[353] John 14:12
[354] See I Thessalonians 4:16; I Corinthians 15:52-53
[355] Ephesians 2:1-6
[356] Ephesians 5:14
[357] Colossians 3:1

The above should not be interpreted as suggesting that we abandon all thoughts of future happenings or glories; for all scriptural passages dealing with the future have important meaning, when rightly understood. At the same time, we should recognize that there is much resurrection work to be accomplished at the present time. There are daily resurrections into which we may enter, and each of these may prove to be a step upward toward some greater attainment. Tennyson wrote:

> "I held it truth, with him who sings
> To one clear harp in divers tones,
> That men may rise on stepping-stones
> Of their dead selves to higher things."

The following quotation should also prove helpful:

"Easter is the celebration of the resurrection of Jesus. Its inner meaning and spiritual significance is the awakening and raising to spiritual consciousness of the I AM in us, which has been dead in trespasses and sins and buried in the tomb of materiality. "I came that they may have life, and may have it abundantly.' The resurrection is the raising up of the whole man—spirit, soul, and body—into the Christ consciousness of life and wholeness. This Jesus did. The tomb could not hold his redeemed perfected body temple. Resurrection is accomplished by the quickening power of the Holy Spirit.

"Every time we rise to the realization of eternal, indwelling life, making union with the Father-Mind, the resurrection of Jesus takes place within us. All thoughts of limitation and inevitable obedience to material law are left in the tomb of materiality".[358]

The Forty Days
Read the passages: John 21:1-25; Luke 24:36-49

The term "forty days" is often applied to the period between Jesus' resurrection and his ascension. Some of the activities during this period have already been discussed, and others are recorded in the Bible passages given above. We should also reread John's Gospel, Chapters Fourteen, Fifteen, Sixteen, and Seventeen—since several of Jesus' statements given in these chapters have important bearing upon this forty-day period.

In scriptural usage the number forty has special significance. Sometimes the reference may be to actual calendar days or years, while at other times an approximate period may be indicated. But in practically every instance the idea to be conveyed by the number forty is the same: That period of time necessary for the completion of the particular activity or piece of work at hand. Thus, the number forty is closely associated with accomplishment.

At this point, therefore, we should try to realize what Jesus was seeking to accomplish during this forty-day period. His purpose was of twofold nature:

Jesus was seeking to establish the truth of his resurrection in the minds of his followers. Apparently, one appearance was not sufficient to accomplish this. Certain fixed beliefs had to be changed, doubts had to be

---

[358] Fillmore, Charles *Keep a True Lent*, p. 197

dissolved, and skeptics had to be convinced. During the forty days all this and much more was accomplished, so that when the Apostles went forth on their preaching mission, they fearlessly proclaimed that "God raised him from the dead, and gave him glory".[359]

Jesus also sought to instruct his followers regarding impending changes—especially those relating to his physical presence. Thus far, Jesus had given personal leadership and had taken the initiative in all activities. But now the Apostles were to assume new responsibilities and were to carry the kingdom message to all parts of the world. Jesus gave them the assurance that he would be with them, but henceforth his leadership would be of a spiritual nature. The forty days, therefore, constituted what may be termed an intermediate period, between the physical and the spiritual presence, preparing the Apostles for the change.

The fullest account of the activities during this forty-day period is found in the twenty-first chapter of John's Gospel. With the explanation given above, this chapter should prove to be of special interest. However, it should be noted that this chapter forms what is often designated as an "appendix" to John's Gospel. As originally written, the Gospel apparently ended with the closing words of the twentieth chapter, and the twenty-first chapter was added (perhaps twenty years later) by another writer. The style of writing and the type of activities mentioned clearly indicate the change of authorship. Also the subject matter reveals the writer's twofold purpose in adding this chapter:

---

[359] I Peter 1:21

The writer feels called upon to explain the passing of the Apostle John, at an advanced age — and to do this in a manner that will not disturb the cherished beliefs of the Early Christians at Ephesus.

The writer also attempts to bolster up some Early Church teachings regarding "the primacy of Peter." These teachings had been somewhat discounted in the earlier part of John's Gospel through the story of the foot-washing.[360] But with the passing of the Apostle John these teachings were apparently making fresh headway, and the writer of this twenty-first chapter seems to be among those favoring the teaching.

However, perhaps the most important feature of the twenty-first chapter is seen in the story of Jesus meeting with his disciples on the shore of Lake Tiberias.[361] We should compare this with an earlier happening, recorded in Luke.[362] Several interesting similarities, and also some differences, will be noted. Both stories point out how discouragement and failure gave place to joy and success when Jesus appeared on the scene. The disciples had "toiled all night," but had accomplished nothing. However, when they obeyed the command of Jesus, their fishing nets were soon filled to overflowing. The story tells how the disciples had been fishing from the "wrong side" of the boat (negative thoughts), with resulting failure. But when they fished from the "right side" (positive thoughts), their efforts were crowned with success!

---

[360] See John 13 with comments in Chapter 10.
[361] See John 21:1-14
[362] Luke 5:1-11

The Ascension

Read the passages: Luke 24:44-53; Acts 1:1-11; Matthew 28:16-20; Mark 16:14-20

Many are familiar with the statement given in the Apostles' Creed: "he ascended into heaven." This statement has reference to the important happening, recorded in the Gospels, which brought the forty-day period of Jesus' ministry to a climactic close. The scriptural passages dealing with Jesus' ascension are given above, and all these should be carefully read, with close attention being paid to the context in each instance.

These accounts of the Ascension form three separate groups, and each group has its special interest:

The Luke-Acts Account

These two sections should be read as forming a continuous story. Luke wrote the Gospel bearing his name, and he also wrote the Acts of the Apostles. The story of the Ascension is begun in Luke and then carried to its conclusion in Acts. It should be recalled that Luke was not a disciple of Jesus, but a convert of the Apostle Paul, so he was not present when the recorded happenings took place. However, in the preface to his Gospel,[363] Luke indicates that he was very careful in gathering and checking the material relating to the activities of Jesus.

Luke gives what is often referred to as "the traditional story of the Ascension." Jesus is shown as parting from his disciples, and then "he was lifted up; and

[363] Luke 1:1-4

a cloud received him out of their sight".[364] In this connection it should also be recalled that Luke was a Gentile, and that his Gospel was written mainly for Gentile Christians. This recognition is important, because at that time the Gentile viewpoint was materialistic, and the recognized deities were regarded as dwelling either on mountaintops or in the skies. Thus, Gentile readers would accept more readily the idea of Jesus coming from and returning to a heavenly abode.

The Mark Account

The closing section of Mark's Gospel[365] is usually referred to as an "appendix." Some versions of the Bible omit this passage altogether, while others call attention to its special nature. There is a possibility that the original ending of Mark's Gospel was lost at a very early period, and this section added by a later writer. An Armenian tradition states that this "appendix" was written by Ariston the Presbyter, who lived early in the second century. Whoever the writer was, he seems to have been familiar with the endings of Matthew and Luke; for in his story of the Ascension he has apparently combined the information given in those Gospels.

The Matthew Account

This passage makes a very important contribution to the story of Jesus' ascension—although for some reason it is often overlooked. Two features in Matthew's story should be specially noted:

---

[364] Acts 1:9
[365] Mark 16:9-20

Matthew was a disciple of Jesus and was actually present at the happening recorded. Note the mention of "the eleven" (disciples)—indicating that the full company of Jesus' disciples was present, with the exception of Judas (who had committed suicide). Thus, we have here the testimony of an "eyewitness."

Matthew also reports that Jesus, after instructing "the eleven" to "make disciples of all nations," gave them this important promise: "I am with you always, even unto the end of the world" (or "consummation of the ages"). It would therefore seem that instead of leaving the disciples, Jesus gave them the assurance of his continued presence. Jesus instructed the disciples to go to all nations; but he would go with them all the way.

Interpreting the Accounts

The Luke and Matthew accounts should not be regarded as contradictory. Rather, we should recognize here the same story, but told from different viewpoints. As already mentioned, Luke wrote for Gentile Christians, who were called upon to face the fact that Jesus was no longer visibly present with them. In their materialistic way of thinking, this could mean only one thing-—that Jesus had gone away to some other place. But Matthew wrote for Jewish Christians, who were accustomed to thinking in spiritual terms. It was not necessary for them to have an image of their God, or any other visible form; his presence with them was fully recognized at all times and under all circumstances. Jewish people recognized that "no man hath seen God at any time";[366] but they also believed that

---

[366] John 1:18

God was "a very present help".[367] Similarly, in regard to the presence of Jesus Christ, there were Christians who needed to "touch and see" before they could believe, as well as those blessed ones "that have not seen, and yet have believed."[368] Thus, for some Christians, Jesus had "gone away"; but others, more spiritually minded, recognized his continuing presence, and they understood Jesus saying, "Abide in me, and I in you".[369]

John's Gospel reports Jesus as saying to Mary, "Touch me not; for I am not yet ascended unto the Father".[370] The word ascended, as here used, can scarcely refer to a departure to take place sometime later. The context indicates that Mary's actions (clinging to Jesus' feet) were tending to hinder some development which was then in process. The Resurrection was an accomplished fact, but a further development was to follow; and apparently Jesus desired that this should be accomplished without further delay. What was the nature of this development?

Thus far, Jesus had demonstrated his divinity in many various ways. His omniscience had been shown through his teaching—for "never man spoke like this man".[371] His omnipotence was revealed through his miracles—his resurrection being the climax. But one further demonstration needed to be made. During his ministry Jesus had apparently limited himself in matters of time and space. It will be recalled that when Jesus came to

---

[367] Psalm 46:1
[368] John 20:26-29
[369] John 15:4
[370] John 20:17
[371] John 7:46

the home of the two sorrowing sisters, Martha said to him, "Lord, if thou had been here, my brother would not have died".[372] But Jesus was not there—for, under human limitations, a person cannot be in two places at one time! Therefore, following the Resurrection, a further demonstration needed to be made. Up to this point Jesus had ministered to the "lost sheep of the House of Israel." Now, since his message of life abundant was to be carried to all the world, he also must be available everywhere — hence, the needed demonstration of omnipresence. When this demonstration was made, no one ever again would be justified in saying, "Jesus was not there!" Instead, no matter what the time, place, or circumstance, there would be the realization of the promise, "I am with you always." Ascension, as applied to Jesus Christ, would thus be understood to mean a continuous demonstration of helpful, life-transforming omnipresence. For the Christian believer it would indicate the attainment of perfect oneness with God.

The following quotations will help to make "this clear:[373]

> *Those who have entered into this process of spiritual evolution, or what Jesus called the regeneration, are prepared for the reception of these divine new ideas, and instead of resisting they say with Jesus, "Not my will, but thine, be done.' This attitude opens the way for the easy advent into their consciousness of God ideas and*

---

[372] John 11:21
[373] Fillmore, Charles *Mysteries of Genesis*, p. 71

leads to an inspiration or steady flow of ideas into it. In this way the sense consciousness is being transformed or lifted up, and the new man appears while the old man is sloughed off. This is crucifixion. The assimilation of the new ideas leads to resurrection and finally to ascension"

We cannot separate Jesus Christ from God or tell where man leaves off and God begins in him. To say that we are men as Jesus Christ was a man is not exactly true, because he had dropped that personal consciousness by which we separate ourselves from our true God self. He became consciously one with the absolute principle of Being. He proved in his resurrection and ascension that he had no consciousness separate from that of Being, therefore he really was this Being to all intents and purposes.

Yet he attained no more than what is expected of every one of us. 'That they may be one, even as we are' was his prayer.

And:[374]

"This is all accomplished through the externalization of the superconsciousness, which is omnipresent and ever ready to manifest itself through us as it did through Jesus. Let 'Christ be formed in you' "

---

[374] Fillmore, Charles Atom Smashing Power of Mind, pp. 40-41

And:[375]

> *Jesus did not leave the planet, at his ascension; he simply entered the inner spiritual realms. He will become visible to those who 'put on Christ' and manifest their incorruptible, undying bodies. Many are conscious of his presence in some degree, but they do not see him as he is, because they have not brought their faculties of apprehension up to his standard. When we awake in his likeness[376] then we shall see him as he is. This does not come about through the soul's leaving the body, but it is accomplished by refining, spiritualizing, and raising both soul and body to higher degrees of power.*

Here we reach the closing point of Part One in this course. Throughout the course we have been considering the activities and teachings of Jesus, covering the period from his birth to his resurrection and ascension. Each step of the way has been recognized as symbolizing a similar step that we may take, as we travel kingdom ward. At this point, therefore, some important statements of Jesus will be appropriate: "Everyone therefore that hears these words of mine, and doeth them, shall be likened unto a wise man, who built his house upon the rock";[377] "My sheep hear my voice, and I know them, and they follow

---

[375] *Metaphysical Bible Dictionary*, p.349
[376] See Psalm 17:15
[377] Matthew 7:24

me: and I give unto them eternal life";[378] "Come, ye blessed of my Father, inherit the kingdom prepared for you from the foundation of the world".[379]

Part Two of this course will deal with the results of Jesus' activities, as the Apostles carried his message "to all the world." The growth and development of apostolic Christianity will be traced step by step, and we will gain a new understanding and appreciation of the Biblical epistles. Therefore, when answers to this lesson have been satisfactorily completed, a fresh start should be made with chapter one of Part Two of this course in the Spiritual study of the Christian Scriptures.

---

[378] John 10:27-28
[379] Matthew 25:34

Chapter 13 – An Epilogue

We have come to the end of our studies of the Christian Gospels and I trust that you have found a number of things that you didn't know or were unsure of. In summary, let's look at a list of things to release:

- An idea of God somewhere, sometimes angry, sometimes benevolent. He is not found in the Gospels. Jesus used a analogy, calling that presence, within everything. Abba... Daddy...
- The idea that everything created as it is now, was created by that creator God in seven literal days. It is clear that the story in Genesis was about a thought, a plan or a dream. The creation of plant life came into being when there was someone to till the soil.[380] The dream is coming forth as we bring the dream into reality.
- The church councils of the fourth and fifth centuries defined Jesus on their own terms, not his. They defined him as God. They did point to the words of John to make their case. But, Jesus stated otherwise. It was Jesus that said, "The Father is greater than I"[381] and "Why call me good? No one is good except God alone!"[382]
- You will not find a resurrection, a hell, a rapture, even a trinity, and many other doctrines in the Gospels. As an example, hell was used to convey

---

[380] Genesis 2:5
[381] John 14:28
[382] John 18:19

symbolically the idea that missing out on the moral vision of the Kingdom of God preached by Jesus and the other prophets was a disaster. In persuasive rhetoric it could be compared to consignment to the smoldering fires of the city dump, Gehenna.

There is much to release in old, inaccurate, mistranslated and misrepresented theology. We trust that what you've discovered in the Gospels is different than what generations of preachers and other clerics have suggested was there and was not.

The Symbol of a "God" working

Better symbols beckon us from the Gospels. There is a treasure trove of symbols there, symbols for a humanity that can level mountains and raise valleys, break chains and part waters. There are symbols for a humanity empowered by courage to start out on a desert of uncharted healing possibilities.

The symbols of resurrection and transfiguration were not events but poetic envisioning of human potential to "make a new heaven and a new earth," to break the grip of what religion paints as our fate, and to see a paradise not as lost but as awaiting our discovery. These poetic symbols have no need of a supernatural super-being that is defined by some as the only way, the only truth and the only life. It is for us to find the way. The way has been pointed out by the mystics of past ages who wrote sacred literature such as the Gospels. It is for us to embrace the Truth and to serve life as no other species in the rest of nature can do.

Appendix A - Parables

An Early Group

1. The Two Houses - Matt. 7:24-27
2. The Two Debtors - Luke 7:41-50
3. The Sower - Matt. 13:1-9 Luke 8:4-8

Parables of the Kingdom

1. The Seed Mark 4:26-29
2. The Tares Matt. 13:24-30
3. The Mustard Seed Matt. 13:31-32 Mark 4:30-32
4. The Leaven Matt. 13:33
5. The Hidden Treasure Matt. 13:44
6. The Costly Pearl Matt. 13:45-46
7. The Fishing Net Matt. 13:47-50
8. The Unforgiving Servant Matt. 18:23-35
9. The Wedding Feast Matt. 22:1-14

The Main Group

1. The Good Samaritan Luke 10:25-37
2. The Empty House Matt. 12:43-45 Luke 11:24-26
3. The Rich Farmer Luke 12:16-21
4. The Barren Fig Tree Luke 13:6-9
5. The Wedding Guest Luke 14:7-11
6. The Lost Sheep Luke 15:1-7
7. The Lost Coin Luke 15:8-10
8. The Prodigal Son Luke 15:11-32
9. The Unjust Steward Luke 16:1-13
10. The Rich Man and Lazarus Luke 16:19-31
11. The Importunate Widow Luke 18:1-8

12. The Pharisee and Publican   Luke 18:9-14
13. The Laborers in the Vineyard Matt. 20:1-16

Parables of Urgent Appeal

1. The Two Sons Matt. 21:28-32
2. The Wicked Husbandmen - Matt. 21:33-46 Mark 12:1-12 Luke 20:9-19
3. The Wedding Feast Matt. 22:1-14 Luke 14:15-24
4. The Ten Virgins
5. The Talents Matt. 25:14-30
6. The Pounds   Luke 19:11-28

Appendix B – Metaphysical Interpretation of Parables

Further Suggestions Concerning Typical Parables

The Sower (Mark 4:1-9)

Setting: Crowds gathered around Jesus, but many persons were motivated only by curiosity, or something similar. What could be done to gain the attention of such persons? Note the way this situation is handled.

Theme: "The importance of receptivity"

Metaphysical Meaning: The "seed" is the freeing word of Truth, and the soil represents our consciousness in varying degrees of receptivity. The "wayside," or pathway, indicates the closed mind, with no receptivity; the "rocky ground" represents shallow thinking or lack of interest, with no lasting receptivity; the "thorns," or weeds, indicate the preoccupied mind. The "good ground" is the receptive mind leading to an abundant harvest. Note the closing emphasis upon the rewards that come to the receptive mind.

The Importunate Widow (Luke 18:1-8)

Setting: Apparently Jesus had been giving some teaching regarding prayer, and questions had arisen about answers to prayer and the tendency to give up if no answers were forthcoming. That this was an oft-discussed subject is shown by many Bible references.[383]

Theme: "Persistence in prayer"

Metaphysical Meaning:

1. The "widow" represents a condition in our experience where something is needed to make life whole and complete.
2. The "judge" represents those conditions or circumstances that seem to hold back our desired good or stand in the way of its manifestation.
3. Note the importance of persistent prayer. Suggested statements for personal use: "Nothing can hold back that which rightfully belongs to me." "I am open and receptive to receive my good." Note the close relationship between faith and persistence. Be careful not to think of the unjust judge as representing God. God does not withhold our good; but persistence is sometimes needed to develop our capacity to receive.

The Prodigal Son (Luke 15:11-32)

Setting: The Jewish leaders were complaining about the attitude of Jesus toward the "publicans and sinners." Jesus' message made a strong appeal to some of these transgressors of the law, and many had already "come to themselves" and were starting life afresh. But apparently the Jewish leaders objected to this rehabilitation work for those whom they regarded as permanent outcasts. It is

---

[383] See Matthew 6:6; Galatians 6:9; I Thessalonians 5:17

easy to recognize these "publicans and sinners" in the "prodigal" and the religious leaders of that day in the "elder brother."

Theme: "The unchanging love of the Father" While this parable has always been known as the parable of the Prodigal Son, it should be noted that it actually deals with the activities of two sons; and the real emphasis is upon the loving and forgiving attitude of the father. The father gave the inheritance to the younger son and then forgave him after "he had spent all." Later the father also forgave the complaining elder brother. The father's love is seen at its best in these activities, and the story clearly points to the forgiving love of God, our Father.

Metaphysical Meaning: The "younger son" represents what is sometimes referred to as "human nature," with its desires of the flesh and the tendency to break away from all supposed restraints of home, seeking its pleasures in the "far country." The "elder brother" represents what may be termed the religious side of our nature; and under certain conditions this may develop a "holier than thou" attitude. However, in both instances a change is possible through repentance. Note how the younger son "came to himself," and there was then a complete change in his thoughts and activities. Above all, recognize the love of the father (as shown in this parable) as a symbol of the forgiving, unchanging love of God, our Heavenly Father; and know that he is ever ready to receive his erring children back into the Father's house.

The Ten Virgins (Matt. 25:1-13)

Setting: Note that this parable belongs to the group designated as "Parables of Urgent Appeal." These parables were spoken by Jesus during the closing period of his ministry, and they indicate his desire that the hearers should give speedy response to the teaching thus presented. Scripture states that "the common people heard him gladly"[384]—but Jesus recognized that there was a wide divergence between "hearing" and "doing"! In some of his earlier messages, Jesus had emphasized this necessity for action, saying, "Not everyone that says unto me, Lord, Lord, shall enter into the kingdom of heaven; but he that doeth the will of my Father".[385] Now the time for action had arrived; and if such action was not taken, the opportunity would pass away.

Theme: "The necessity for preparedness"

Metaphysical Meaning: Several important points should be carefully considered:

1. The "virgins" are sometimes regarded as representing our faculties, some of which may be alert and ready for advancement, while others may have fallen asleep.
2. The attitude of some of the virgins in refusing to share their oil has often been questioned, and on first reading this attitude does seem contrary to Christian teaching. However, we must recognize that there are some things and experiences in life

---

[384] Mark 12:37
[385] Matthew 7:21

which cannot be shared. The "oil" mentioned is suggestive of the possibilities of spiritual illumination—an individual experience which each person must seek and find for himself. The "foolish virgins" had time and opportunity to obtain this "oil," but they chose to spend their time in sleep.

3. "Behold, the bridegroom!" This call comes to all persons, in many ways and at many times, and the call represents life's supreme opportunity. Then it is that prepared men and women are able to enter the festive chamber and join with the bridegroom in the joys of the wedding feast; but those who are unprepared find themselves facing the closed door. It is significant that shortly before giving this parable, Jesus had uttered the memorable words: "O Jerusalem, Jerusalem ... how often would I have gathered thy children together, even as a hen gathers her chickens under her wings, and ye would not!".[386]

---

[386] Matthew 23:37

Appendix C - The Healing Miracles of Jesus

Section 1, Gospel of Matthew
1. Simon's Mother-in-law Matthew 8:14-15; Mark 1:30-31; Luke 4:38-39
2. A Leper Matthew 8:2-4; Mark 1:40-45 Luke 5:12-14
3. The Centurion's Servant Matthew 8:5-13; Luke 7:1-10
4. The Afflicted Woman Matt. 9:20-22; Mark 5:25-34; Luke 8:43-48
5. Two Blind Men Matthew 9:27-34
6. Man with Withered Hand Matthew 12:9-14; Mark 3:1-6; Luke 6:6-11
7. The Syrophoenician Woman's Daughter Matt. 15:21-28; Mark 7:24-30

Section 2, Gospel of Mark
1. Man with Unclean Spirit Mark 1:23-26; Luke 4:33-35
2. A Paralytic Mark 2:1-12; Matt. 9:2-8; Luke 5:17-26
3. Man: Dumb, Blind Mark 3:22; Matt. 12:22-24
4. The Gadarene Demoniac Mark 5:1-20; Matt. 8:28-34; Luke 8:26-39
5. Man: Deaf, Dumb Mark 7:31-37; Matt. 15:29-31
6. Blind Man, Bethsaida Mark 8:22-26
7. Epileptic Boy Mark 9:14-29; Matt. 17:14-20; Luke 9:37-43

Section 3, Gospel of Luke
1. The Dumb Demoniac Luke 11:14
2. The Crippled Woman Luke 13:10-21
3. Man with Dropsy Luke 14:1-6
4. The Ten Lepers Luke 17:11-19

5. Blind Man, Jericho Luke 18:35-43; Matt. 20:29-34; Mark 10:46-52
6. Malchus' Ear Luke 22:49-51; Matt. 26:50-51; Mark 14:47

Section 4. Gospel of John

1. The Nobleman's Son John 4:46-54
2. The Impotent Man John 5:1-16
3. The Man Born Blind John 9:1-41

Jesus' Miracles of Supply

1. Water Made Wine John 2:1-11
2. Draught of Fishes Luke 5:1-11
3. Feeding Five Thousand Matt. 14:13-23; John 6:1-15 Mark 6:30-46; Luke 9:10-17
4. Feeding Four Thousand Matt. 15:32-38; Mark 8:1-9
5. Tax Money Matt. 17:24-27
6. Draught of Fishes John 21:6-11

Jesus' Miracles Overcoming Death

1. Widow's Son, Nain Luke 7:11-17
2. Jairus' Daughter Matt. 9:18-26; Mark 5:21-43; Luke 8:40-56)
3. Raising of Lazarus John 11:1-46

Jesus' "Nature" Miracles

1. Stilling the Storm Matt. 8:23-27; Mark 4:35-41; Luke 8:22-25
2. Walking on Water Matt. 14:24-26; Mark 6:47-56; John 6:16-21
3. Withered Fig Tree Matt. 21:18-22; Mark 11:20-25

Index

Unity of Northern Colorado Publications

This publication is one in a series on Unity School of Religious Studies subjects. We also have:

- *Spiritual Interpretation of the Hebrew Scriptures*
- *Spiritual Interpretation of the Christian Scriptures: The Gospels*
- *Spiritual Interpretation of the Christian Scriptures: Acts – Revelation*
- *Revelation – A Metaphysical Interpretation*
- *Unity Metaphysics*

The following book is a collection of quotutions from Unity Books through 1984:

- *Quotable Quotes from Unity Books*

We have a series on the work of Classic New Thought writers. These publications include:

- *The Impersonal Life* – Joseph Benner
- *The Game of Life and How to Play It* – Florence Scovell Shinn
- *The Power of Awareness* – Neville Goddard
- *The Twelve Powers* – Charles Fillmore
- *Lessons in Truth* – H. Emilie Cady

Other books are available based on classes at Unity Spiritual Center (Arizona) and Unity of Northern Colorado. They include:

- *Christianity: A History*

- *A Country that Works for All*
- *A Course in Abundance*
- *A Course in Consciousness*
- *The Devine Feminine*
- *Discovering Unity*
- *Effective Ministry Leadership* (with Jill Campbell)
- *Perception*
- *A Practical Life with a Powerful Purpose* (with Sharon Bush)
- *Religion vs. Homosexuality*
- *A Spiritual Introduction to the World's Religions* (with Sharon Bush)
- *Thought*
- *Is Unity a Cult?*

The following is a collection of Rev. Jim's Lessons:

- *What You Seek is Seeking You*

The following publication includes a CD with a searchable database on writings from many faith traditions:

- *Wisdom of the Ages*

These publications are available on Amazon as well as Unity of Northern Colorado. See additional information and other resources at our website: www.unitynoco.org

Unity of Northern Colorado Online Classes

The class presented in this book and other classes are available, without charge, via Zoom. See our website for start dates and other information.

Made in the USA
Middletown, DE
09 January 2023

21691309R00156